Shadow Codes

The Master Spy of the Digital Age

Copyright © 2024 by RK Books

All rights reserved.

No part of this publication may be reproduced, distributed, or transmitted in any form or by any means, including photocopying, recording, or other electronic or mechanical methods, without the prior written permission of the publisher, except in the case of brief quotations embodied in critical reviews and certain other noncommercial uses permitted by copyright law.

This book is a work of fiction. Names, characters, places, and incidents are products of the author's imagination or are used fictitiously. Any resemblance to actual events, locales, or persons, living or dead, is entirely coincidental.

ISBN: 978-969-459-260-2   Ebook

ISBN: 978-969-459-261-9   Paper-Back

ISBN: 978-969-459-262-6   Hard-Back

Published by |

Table of Contents

Introduction 1

Chapter 1 Understanding Cyber Spying 4

    What is Cyber Spying? 5

    Why Cyber Spying Matters 7

    How Cyber Spying Affects You 11

Chapter 2 How Cyber Spying Started 15

    Cold War Origins 16

    Transition to the Digital Age 19

    Pioneers of Cyber Espionage 22

Chapter 3 Becoming a Master Spy in the Digital World 26

    Skills Needed for Cyber Spying 27

    Training and Recruitment 29

    The Rise of Digital Masterminds 33

Chapter 4 Tools Cyber Spies Use 37

    Malware and Viruses 37

    Hacking Techniques 43

    Surveillance Technology 46

Chapter 5 Types of Cyber Spies 51

    State-Sponsored Spies 51

    Hacktivists 56

    Cyber criminals 61

Chapter 6 Tricks Cyber Spies Use to Trick People 67

    Phishing Attacks 67

    Social Engineering 72

    Spoofing and Impersonation 77

Chapter 7 Who Cyber Spies Target 84
    Government Agencies 84
    Corporations.. 90
    Individuals and Privacy 96
Chapter 8 How Cyber Spies Gather Information? 102
    Data Collection Methods... 102
    Cyber Surveillance 107
    Exploiting Vulnerabilities 113
Chapter 9 Nations Competing in Cyber Spying 119
    Global Cyber Powers 120
    Cyber Arms Race 125
    The Impact on International Relations.................................... 131
Chapter 10 Exploring the Dark Web 135
    What is the Dark Web? 136
    Cyber Spying on the Dark Web.. 141

Introduction

In the shadows of the digital world lies a realm unseen but profoundly impactful - the domain of cyber espionage. Welcome to "Shadow Codes: The Master Spy of the Digital Age." In this exploration, we delve into the clandestine operations, intricate techniques, and profound implications of cyber spying in the modern era.

The digital age has birthed a new breed of spies - individuals and organizations adept at navigating the complexities of cyberspace to infiltrate, gather intelligence, and disrupt operations of adversaries. Gone are the days of trench coats and hidden microphones; today's spies wield keyboards and lines of code to accomplish their objectives. They are the masters of the unseen, the architects of virtual intrigue, and the shadowy figures behind the curtain of ones and zeros.

The title "Shadow Codes" captures the essence of this clandestine world, where information is currency, and encryption is the language of secrecy. Behind every digital transaction, communication, and interaction, lurks the potential for surveillance, manipulation, and exploitation. These shadow codes, hidden within the vast expanse of the internet, hold the keys to unlocking secrets, influencing decisions, and shaping destinies.

But who are these master spies of the digital age? They come in various forms - from state-sponsored hackers targeting rival nations' infrastructure to cybercriminal syndicates seeking financial gain, and from hacktivist groups advocating for political change to lone wolves driven by personal vendettas. Their motivations are as diverse as their methods, yet they share a common goal: to wield the power of information to achieve their objectives.

As we embark on this journey into the world of cyber espionage, we must confront the reality that the digital landscape is not just a playground for innovation and connectivity but also a battleground for espionage and warfare. The interconnectedness of our modern society has created unprecedented opportunities for surveillance and exploitation, challenging traditional notions of security and privacy.

In "Shadow Codes," we will peel back the layers of this clandestine world, exploring the tools, tactics, and targets of cyber spies. We will uncover the inner workings of malware, phishing schemes, and social engineering tactics used to breach defenses and infiltrate networks. We will shine a light on the dark web, the underground marketplace where illicit activities flourish and anonymity reigns supreme.

But beyond the technical aspects, we will also examine the ethical implications of cyber espionage. In an age where personal data is currency and surveillance is ubiquitous, where do we draw the line between security and privacy? How do we hold accountable those who exploit vulnerabilities for nefarious purposes? These are questions that demand our attention as we navigate the murky waters of the digital age.

Ultimately, "Shadow Codes" is not just a book about cyber espionage; it is a reflection of the complex interplay between technology, power, and ethics in the modern world. It is a call to action for vigilance, transparency, and accountability in an era defined by shadows and secrets. Join us as we shine a light on the master spies of the digital age and uncover the secrets hidden within the shadow codes.

Chapter 1

Understanding Cyber Spying

Welcome to the world of cyber spying, where the battleground is not marked by physical borders but by digital ones. In this chapter, we embark on a journey to understand the fundamental concepts of cyber espionage - the clandestine art of gathering intelligence, disrupting operations, and exerting influence in the digital realm.

Cyber spying, also known as cyber espionage, encompasses a wide array of activities conducted by individuals, organizations, and governments to gain unauthorized access to sensitive information, manipulate data, or sabotage systems for strategic advantage. Unlike traditional espionage, which often involved physical infiltration and covert operations, cyber spying leverages technology and networks to achieve its objectives, making it both elusive and pervasive in the digital age.

At its core, cyber spying revolves around the exploitation of vulnerabilities in computer systems, networks, and software to steal, manipulate, or disrupt data. From sophisticated nation-state actors targeting rival governments' infrastructure to lone hackers seeking financial gain, the motivations behind cyber espionage are as diverse as the actors themselves. Understanding the dynamics of cyber spying is essential in navigating the complexities of the digital landscape and safeguarding against potential threats. Join us as we delve deeper into the world of cyber espionage and uncover the tactics, techniques, and implications of this shadowy endeavor.

What is Cyber Spying?

Cyber spying, also known as cyber espionage, is a clandestine practice wherein individuals, organizations, or governments seek to covertly gather intelligence, manipulate data, or disrupt operations of adversaries using digital means. In the interconnected world of cyberspace, where information flows freely and digital systems pervade every aspect of modern life, cyber spying has emerged as a powerful tool for surveillance, espionage, and coercion. Understanding the nature, methods, and implications of cyber spying is essential in navigating the complexities of the digital landscape and safeguarding against potential threats.

At its core, cyber spying involves the unauthorized access to and exploitation of computer systems, networks, and software to gain valuable information or advantage. Unlike traditional espionage, which often relied on physical infiltration and covert operations, cyber spying leverages technology and the internet to achieve its objectives, making it both elusive and pervasive in the digital age. While the motivations behind cyber spying vary widely, they often include national security interests, economic espionage, political influence, or personal gain.

One of the defining characteristics of cyber spying is its covert nature. Unlike traditional forms of espionage, cyber spies operate in the shadows of the digital realm, using sophisticated techniques and technologies to conceal their activities and evade detection. This clandestine approach allows cyber spies to gather intelligence, manipulate data, or sabotage systems without alerting their targets or leaving behind physical evidence.

Cyber spies employ a wide range of tactics and techniques to achieve their objectives. One common method is the use of malware, malicious software designed to infiltrate and compromise computer systems or networks. Malware can take many forms, including viruses, worms, trojans, and ransomware, each with its own capabilities and purposes. Once installed on a target system, malware can exfiltrate sensitive data, monitor user activity, or even disrupt critical operations.

Phishing is another prevalent tactic used by cyber spies to deceive and manipulate their targets. Phishing involves sending fraudulent emails or messages that appear to be from a legitimate source, such as a trusted organization or individual. These messages often contain malicious links or attachments designed to trick recipients into revealing sensitive information, such as passwords, financial data, or personal details. By exploiting human psychology and trust, phishing attacks can be highly effective in gaining unauthorized access to systems or compromising user accounts.

Social engineering is yet another technique commonly employed by cyber spies to manipulate individuals or organizations into divulging confidential information or performing actions that benefit the attacker. Social engineering tactics may include pretexting, where the attacker impersonates a trusted individual or authority figure to gain access to sensitive information, or baiting, where the attacker lures victims into downloading malware or disclosing passwords by offering enticing rewards or incentives.

In addition to these tactics, cyber spies may also exploit vulnerabilities in software, networks, or infrastructure to gain unauthorized access to systems or compromise security. Vulnerability exploitation involves identifying and exploiting weaknesses or flaws in software code, network configurations, or system architecture to gain privileged access or execute malicious code. Zero-day vulnerabilities, in particular, pose a significant threat as they are unknown to the software vendor and remain unpatched, leaving systems vulnerable to exploitation by cyber attackers.

The implications of cyber spying are far-reaching and multifaceted. On a geopolitical level, cyber espionage can disrupt diplomatic relations, undermine national security, and escalate tensions between nations. State-sponsored cyber attacks, such as those targeting government agencies, military infrastructure, or critical infrastructure, can have devastating consequences, including loss of life, economic damage, and political instability.

Economically, cyber espionage poses a significant threat to businesses, industries, and economies worldwide. Intellectual property theft, industrial espionage, and economic espionage can result in billions of dollars in losses for companies and undermine innovation, competitiveness, and economic growth. Additionally, cyber espionage targeting financial institutions, online retailers, or cryptocurrency exchanges can compromise consumer confidence, disrupt markets, and erode trust in digital commerce.

Individually, cyber espionage can have profound implications for privacy, security, and personal safety. Data breaches, identity theft, and cyber stalking are just a few examples of the risks posed by cyber spying to individuals and communities. Moreover, the proliferation of surveillance technologies, data collection practices, and online tracking mechanisms raises concerns about the erosion of privacy rights and civil liberties in the digital age.

Cyber spying represents a pervasive and evolving threat in the digital age. With the increasing interconnectedness of our society and reliance on technology, the risks posed by cyber espionage are greater than ever before. By understanding the nature, methods, and implications of cyber spying, individuals, organizations, and governments can better protect themselves against this shadowy menace and safeguard the integrity, security, and resilience of cyberspace for future generations.

Why Cyber Spying Matters

Cyber spying matters profoundly in the modern world due to its far-reaching implications for national security, economic stability, individual privacy, and global geopolitics. As technology continues to advance and societies become increasingly interconnected, the risks posed by cyber espionage have become more significant than ever before. Understanding why cyber spying matters requires a comprehensive examination of its impact across various domains.

1. **National Security:** Perhaps the most critical aspect of why cyber spying matters is its profound impact on national security. Nation-states engage in cyber espionage to gather intelligence, monitor adversaries, and gain strategic advantages in conflicts. State-sponsored cyber attacks targeting government agencies, military infrastructure, or critical national infrastructure pose a significant threat to a nation's sovereignty, stability, and defense capabilities. For example, cyber spies may seek to steal classified information, sabotage critical systems, or disrupt essential services, leading to potential loss of life, economic damage, and political instability. The ability to defend against cyber espionage is paramount to ensuring the security and resilience of nations in an increasingly digitized world.

2. **Economic Espionage:** Cyber spying also matters significantly in the context of economic stability and prosperity. Nation-states and corporate entities engage in economic espionage to steal intellectual property, trade secrets, and proprietary information for competitive advantage. By infiltrating rival companies' networks or targeting research institutions, cyber spies can gain access to valuable technology, research, and innovation, undermining the economic competitiveness and innovation ecosystem of targeted nations. Economic espionage can result in billions of dollars in losses for companies, hinder technological progress, and erode trust in business partnerships and trade relations. Protecting against economic espionage is crucial for fostering innovation, fostering economic growth, and safeguarding intellectual property rights.

3. **Political Influence:** Cyber spying plays a pivotal role in shaping political landscapes, influencing elections, and manipulating public opinion. State-sponsored cyber operations, such as disinformation campaigns, propaganda efforts, and election interference, seek to undermine democratic processes, sow discord, and amplify political divisions within targeted nations. By spreading false information, amplifying extremist viewpoints, or exploiting social media platforms, cyber spies can manipulate public perceptions, sway voter sentiments, and undermine trust in democratic institutions. Political influence campaigns conducted through cyber espionage pose a significant threat to the integrity of democratic systems, social cohesion, and national unity. Protecting against political influence operations requires enhancing transparency, promoting media literacy, and bolstering cybersecurity defenses to safeguard against manipulation and misinformation.

4. **Critical Infrastructure Protection:** Cyber spying also matters concerning the protection of critical infrastructure, such as energy grids, transportation networks, and healthcare systems. State-sponsored cyber attacks targeting critical infrastructure can have devastating consequences, including disruptions to essential services, economic disruptions, and public safety risks. By infiltrating industrial control systems, exploiting vulnerabilities in network infrastructure, or launching denial-of-service attacks, cyber spies can disrupt operations, cause physical damage, and compromise public safety. Protecting critical infrastructure against cyber espionage requires collaboration between government agencies, private sector entities, and international partners to identify vulnerabilities, enhance resilience, and mitigate risks effectively.

5. **Individual Privacy:** Cyber spying poses a significant threat to individual privacy rights, personal autonomy, and digital

freedoms. Surveillance technologies, data collection practices, and online tracking mechanisms employed by cyber spies can intrude upon individuals' privacy, monitor their activities, and undermine their rights to anonymity and free expression. Mass surveillance programs conducted by governments, data breaches by malicious actors, and corporate data harvesting practices raise concerns about the erosion of privacy rights in the digital age. Protecting individual privacy requires robust legal frameworks, technological safeguards, and ethical guidelines to ensure that individuals' personal data is handled responsibly, transparently, and with due regard for their rights and freedoms.

6. **Global Geopolitics:** Finally, cyber spying matters in the context of global geopolitics, international relations, and diplomatic affairs. Cyber espionage activities conducted by nation-states can exacerbate tensions, escalate conflicts, and destabilize regions worldwide. State-sponsored cyber attacks targeting foreign governments, military installations, or critical infrastructure can trigger diplomatic crises, provoke retaliatory measures, and lead to escalation in cyber warfare. The proliferation of offensive cyber capabilities, the lack of international norms and regulations governing cyber espionage, and the absence of effective deterrence mechanisms pose significant challenges to global security and stability. Addressing cyber spying in the context of geopolitics requires fostering international cooperation, establishing norms of behavior, and developing mechanisms for attribution, accountability, and dispute resolution.

Cyber spying matters profoundly in the modern world due to its far-reaching implications for national security, economic stability, individual privacy, and global geopolitics. By understanding the nature, methods, and implications of cyber espionage, individuals, organizations, and governments can better protect themselves against this pervasive threat and safeguard the integrity, security, and resilience of cyberspace for future generations. Efforts to address cyber spying require a multi-faceted approach encompassing technological innovation, legal reform, international cooperation, and public awareness to mitigate risks effectively and promote a safe, secure, and trustworthy digital environment for all.

How Cyber Spying Affects You

Understanding how cyber spying affects individuals is crucial in navigating the complexities of the digital age. From threats to personal privacy and security to broader societal impacts, cyber espionage has far-reaching consequences that can profoundly impact people's lives in various ways.

1. **Privacy Concerns:** One of the most immediate ways cyber spying affects individuals is through privacy concerns. With the proliferation of surveillance technologies, data collection practices, and online tracking mechanisms, individuals' personal information is increasingly vulnerable to unauthorized access, monitoring, and exploitation. State-sponsored surveillance programs, corporate data harvesting practices, and malicious hacking activities pose significant threats to individual privacy rights, autonomy, and digital freedoms. For example, the collection of metadata by government agencies, the use of tracking cookies by advertisers, and the exposure of personal data in data breaches can all compromise individuals' privacy and expose them to potential harm.

2. **Identity Theft and Fraud:** Cyber spying also puts individuals at risk of identity theft, fraud, and financial exploitation. Malicious actors may use stolen personal information, such as Social Security numbers, credit card details, or login credentials, to impersonate individuals, conduct fraudulent transactions, or

steal their assets. Phishing attacks, malware infections, and data breaches can all facilitate identity theft and fraud schemes, leading to financial losses, reputational damage, and emotional distress for victims. Protecting against identity theft and fraud requires vigilance, awareness, and proactive measures, such as using strong passwords, enabling two-factor authentication, and monitoring financial accounts for suspicious activity.

3. **Surveillance and Monitoring:** Individuals may also be subject to surveillance and monitoring by governments, corporations, or malicious actors engaged in cyber spying activities. Surveillance technologies, such as closed-circuit television (CCTV) cameras, facial recognition systems, and electronic monitoring devices, can track individuals' movements, behaviors, and activities in public and private spaces. Similarly, online surveillance techniques, such as internet monitoring, social media tracking, and email interception, can invade individuals' digital privacy and expose them to potential scrutiny or manipulation. The pervasive nature of surveillance and monitoring in the digital age raises concerns about civil liberties, human rights, and the right to privacy, prompting calls for greater transparency, accountability, and oversight of surveillance practices.

4. **Cyber Stalking and Harassment:** Cyber spying can also manifest in the form of cyber stalking, harassment, and online abuse directed at individuals. Malicious actors may use social media platforms, messaging apps, or email to harass, intimidate, or threaten their victims, causing emotional distress, psychological trauma, and social isolation. Cyber stalking behaviors, such as persistent monitoring, unwanted contact, and dissemination of personal information, can escalate into real-world threats and violence, posing serious risks to individuals' safety and well-being. Combatting cyber stalking and

harassment requires legal protections, law enforcement intervention, and support services for victims to ensure their safety, security, and dignity in online spaces.

5. **Data Privacy and Consent:** Individuals' data privacy and consent rights are also implicated in cyber spying activities, particularly in the context of data collection, processing, and sharing practices. Companies and organizations often collect vast amounts of personal data from individuals through various online services, applications, and platforms, often without their explicit consent or awareness. This data may be used for targeted advertising, behavioral profiling, or algorithmic decision-making, raising concerns about individual autonomy, consent, and control over personal information. The lack of transparency, accountability, and regulatory oversight in data privacy practices exacerbates these concerns, necessitating greater regulation, accountability, and user empowerment to protect individuals' data privacy rights.

6. **Psychological Impact:** Beyond the tangible harms of cyber spying, individuals may also experience psychological impacts, such as anxiety, stress, and paranoia, as a result of perceived surveillance, monitoring, or exposure to online threats. The constant awareness of potential privacy violations, data breaches, or cyber attacks can contribute to feelings of vulnerability, insecurity, and distrust in digital interactions. Additionally, the fear of being surveilled or targeted by malicious actors may lead individuals to self-censorship, avoidance of online activities, or disengagement from digital platforms, limiting their participation in online communities and social networks. Addressing the psychological impacts of cyber spying requires fostering digital literacy, promoting resilience, and providing support services for individuals affected by online threats and harassment.

Cyber spying affects individuals in myriad ways, from threats to personal privacy and security to broader societal impacts on civil liberties, human rights, and psychological well-being. By understanding the nature, methods, and implications of cyber espionage, individuals can better protect themselves against online threats and advocate for greater transparency, accountability, and ethical standards in digital practices. Efforts to address cyber spying require a multi-faceted approach encompassing legal reform, technological innovation, public education, and international cooperation to promote a safe, secure, and trustworthy digital environment for all.

Chapter 2
How Cyber Spying Started

The origins of cyber spying can be traced back to the early days of computing, when the emergence of digital technologies presented new opportunities and challenges for intelligence gathering and surveillance. In this chapter, we delve into the historical context and key milestones that marked the beginning of cyber espionage, from the Cold War era to the advent of the internet age.

As the world entered the Cold War period, intelligence agencies began to recognize the potential of computers and telecommunications technologies for espionage and surveillance purposes. The rapid advancements in computing capabilities, coupled with the growing interconnectedness of global communication networks, created new avenues for gathering intelligence, monitoring adversaries, and conducting covert operations.

During the Cold War, both the United States and the Soviet Union invested heavily in developing sophisticated surveillance and espionage capabilities, leveraging emerging technologies such as cryptography, signal intelligence, and satellite reconnaissance. The Space Race, the Arms Race, and geopolitical tensions fueled a competition for technological supremacy and strategic advantage, driving innovations in cyber espionage techniques and tactics.

With the proliferation of personal computers, the internet, and digital communications in the late 20th century, cyber spying entered a new phase of evolution, characterized by increased connectivity, complexity, and sophistication. The digitization of information, the globalization of commerce, and the rise of cybercrime presented new challenges and opportunities for intelligence agencies, governments, and malicious actors alike.

Cold War Origins

The Cold War, spanning roughly from the end of World War II in 1945 to the dissolution of the Soviet Union in 1991, was characterized by intense geopolitical rivalry and ideological confrontation between the United States and the Soviet Union. Central to this conflict was the struggle for global supremacy in political, economic, and military spheres, which played out on multiple fronts, including espionage and intelligence gathering. The Cold War era marked the beginning of modern cyber spying, as both superpowers recognized the strategic importance of information technology and telecommunications for national security and intelligence purposes.

1. **Origins of Cyber Spying:** The origins of cyber spying during the Cold War can be traced back to the early efforts of intelligence agencies to harness emerging technologies for espionage and surveillance. The development of computers, telecommunications networks, and cryptography during this period provided new tools and capabilities for gathering intelligence, monitoring communications, and conducting covert operations. Both the United States and the Soviet Union invested heavily in building sophisticated intelligence infrastructure and capabilities, including signals intelligence (SIGINT), codebreaking, and covert surveillance operations.

2. **Signal Intelligence (SIGINT):** Signal intelligence, or SIGINT, played a central role in Cold War-era cyber spying efforts. SIGINT involves intercepting and analyzing electronic signals, such as radio transmissions, telephone conversations, and digital communications, to gather intelligence about enemy activities,

intentions, and capabilities. Intelligence agencies, such as the National Security Agency (NSA) in the United States and the KGB in the Soviet Union, developed extensive SIGINT capabilities to monitor communications between government officials, military units, and diplomatic missions, providing valuable insights into enemy plans and intentions.

3. **Codebreaking and Cryptography:** Codebreaking and cryptography were critical components of Cold War-era cyber spying operations. Both the United States and the Soviet Union invested heavily in developing cryptographic technologies and techniques to encrypt and decrypt sensitive communications. The NSA, in particular, played a key role in breaking enemy codes and ciphers, such as the Enigma machine used by Nazi Germany during World War II. Cryptanalysis, the science of breaking codes and ciphers, became a major focus of intelligence agencies' efforts to gain access to enemy communications and intelligence.

4. **Covert Surveillance Operations:** Covert surveillance operations were another hallmark of Cold War-era cyber spying. Intelligence agencies conducted clandestine operations to infiltrate enemy organizations, monitor diplomatic communications, and gather intelligence on enemy activities. The CIA and KGB both ran extensive networks of agents, informants, and operatives around the world to collect information, recruit assets, and conduct covert operations. These operations often involved sophisticated tradecraft, including disguises, dead drops, and covert communication methods, to evade detection and maintain operational security.

5. **Technological Innovations:** The Cold War era witnessed rapid advancements in technology that revolutionized the field of cyber spying. The development of computers, miniaturized electronics, and telecommunications networks provided new

opportunities for intelligence gathering and surveillance. The invention of the transistor, integrated circuits, and microprocessors enabled the miniaturization of electronic devices, making it possible to build smaller, more powerful surveillance equipment. The proliferation of satellites, reconnaissance aircraft, and surveillance drones also enhanced the capabilities of intelligence agencies to gather imagery and signals intelligence from remote locations.

6. **Espionage and Counterintelligence:** Espionage and counterintelligence were central aspects of Cold War-era cyber spying efforts. Both the United States and the Soviet Union engaged in extensive espionage operations to infiltrate each other's governments, military organizations, and scientific institutions. Double agents, moles, and sleeper cells were deployed to gather intelligence, sabotage enemy operations, and sow disinformation. Counterintelligence agencies, such as the FBI and KGB, worked tirelessly to identify and neutralize enemy spies, prevent leaks of classified information, and protect national security interests.

The Cold War era marked the beginning of modern cyber spying, as both the United States and the Soviet Union recognized the strategic importance of information technology and telecommunications for intelligence gathering and surveillance. The development of signal intelligence, codebreaking, covert surveillance operations, and technological innovations laid the foundation for the cyber spying capabilities that would continue to evolve and expand in the decades to come. By understanding the origins of cyber spying during the Cold War, we can gain valuable insights into the motivations, methods, and implications of modern cyber espionage in the digital age.

Transition to the Digital Age

The transition to the digital age marked a significant shift in the landscape of cyber spying, as advancements in computing, telecommunications, and information technology revolutionized the methods, capabilities, and implications of intelligence gathering and surveillance. From the late 20th century onwards, the proliferation of personal computers, the internet, and digital communication networks created new opportunities and challenges for cyber spies, governments, and malicious actors alike. Understanding this transition is crucial in comprehending the evolution of cyber espionage and its profound impact on modern society.

1. **Emergence of Personal Computing:** The transition to the digital age was catalyzed by the emergence of personal computing in the late 20th century. The invention of the microprocessor, the development of operating systems, and the commercialization of personal computers enabled individuals and organizations to access, process, and store vast amounts of data with unprecedented speed and efficiency. Personal computers became ubiquitous in homes, businesses, and government agencies, transforming the way people work, communicate, and interact with information.

2. **Proliferation of the Internet:** The advent of the internet revolutionized the way people access, share, and exchange information, creating new opportunities for communication, commerce, and collaboration on a global scale. The development of the World Wide Web, hypertext markup language (HTML), and web browsers made it easy for users to navigate and interact with digital content online. The internet also facilitated the rapid dissemination of information, enabling individuals and organizations to communicate instantaneously and access a wealth of resources and services from anywhere in the world.

3. **Global Connectivity and Interdependence:** The internet's global connectivity and interdependence brought people, businesses, and governments closer together but also created new vulnerabilities and risks. The interconnected nature of cyberspace made it possible for cyber spies to conduct espionage and surveillance activities on a global scale, targeting individuals, organizations, and governments from remote locations. The borderless nature of the internet blurred the lines between domestic and international cyber threats, challenging traditional notions of sovereignty, jurisdiction, and accountability.

4. **Rise of Cyber Warfare:** The transition to the digital age also witnessed the rise of cyber warfare as a new domain of conflict and competition between nations. State-sponsored cyber attacks targeting government agencies, military installations, and critical infrastructure became increasingly common, as nations sought to gain strategic advantages and assert their influence in cyberspace. The Stuxnet worm, believed to be developed by the United States and Israel, was one of the first known instances of a cyber weapon being used to sabotage an adversary's nuclear program, signaling the emergence of a new era of warfare.

5. **Cyber Espionage and Intelligence Gathering:** The digital age provided cyber spies with new tools and techniques for gathering intelligence and conducting surveillance operations. The internet's vast trove of digital data, including emails, documents, and social media posts, became a rich source of information for intelligence agencies seeking to monitor adversaries, identify threats, and gather insights into enemy activities. Signals intelligence (SIGINT) capabilities expanded to encompass digital communications, such as email, instant messaging, and Voice over Internet Protocol (VoIP), enabling

cyber spies to intercept and analyze electronic signals in real-time.

6. **Technological Advancements and Innovations:**
Technological advancements and innovations fueled the evolution of cyber spying capabilities during the transition to the digital age. The development of advanced encryption algorithms, secure communication protocols, and cryptographic techniques strengthened the security of digital communications and made it more difficult for cyber spies to intercept and decrypt sensitive information. Conversely, the proliferation of malware, hacking tools, and exploit kits provided malicious actors with new means of infiltrating computer systems, stealing data, and disrupting operations.

7. **Challenges and Risks:** The transition to the digital age also brought new challenges and risks for cybersecurity and national security. The increasing reliance on digital technologies and interconnected systems made individuals, organizations, and governments more vulnerable to cyber attacks, data breaches, and information warfare. Nation-states, criminal syndicates, and hacktivist groups exploited vulnerabilities in software, networks, and infrastructure to launch a wide range of cyber threats, including ransomware attacks, distributed denial-of-service (DDoS) attacks, and data thefts.

8. **Regulatory and Policy Responses:** Governments and policymakers responded to the challenges of the digital age by enacting laws, regulations, and policies aimed at enhancing cybersecurity, protecting critical infrastructure, and combating cyber threats. The European Union's General Data Protection Regulation (GDPR), for example, introduced stringent data protection requirements and penalties for non-compliance, while the United States established agencies such as the Department of Homeland Security (DHS) and the Cybersecurity and

Infrastructure Security Agency (CISA) to coordinate cybersecurity efforts and protect national critical infrastructure.

The transition to the digital age marked a profound shift in the landscape of cyber spying, as advancements in computing, telecommunications, and information technology transformed the methods, capabilities, and implications of intelligence gathering and surveillance. The emergence of personal computing, the proliferation of the internet, and the rise of cyber warfare reshaped the geopolitical landscape, challenging traditional notions of security, sovereignty, and privacy. By understanding this transition, we can gain valuable insights into the evolution of cyber espionage and its profound impact on modern society.

Pioneers of Cyber Espionage

Pioneers of cyber espionage played pivotal roles in shaping the landscape of intelligence gathering and surveillance in the digital age. These individuals and organizations were early adopters of emerging technologies, innovators in covert operations, and trailblazers in exploiting the potential of cyberspace for espionage purposes. Their contributions laid the foundation for modern cyber spying capabilities and influenced the evolution of cyber espionage tactics, techniques, and strategies.

1. **National Security Agency (NSA):** The NSA, established in 1952, played a pioneering role in signals intelligence (SIGINT) and codebreaking during the Cold War era. With a mandate to intercept, analyze, and exploit foreign communications, the NSA developed sophisticated surveillance capabilities to monitor enemy communications, decrypt encrypted messages, and gather intelligence on adversary activities. The NSA's success in breaking enemy codes and ciphers, such as the Enigma machine used by Nazi Germany during World War II, established it as a world leader in cryptanalysis and electronic surveillance.

2. **Government Communications Headquarters (GCHQ):** The GCHQ, Britain's signals intelligence agency, has been at the forefront of cyber espionage and surveillance efforts since its establishment in 1919. With a focus on intercepting and analyzing foreign communications, the GCHQ played a key role in decrypting enemy codes and ciphers during World War II and the Cold War. In the digital age, the GCHQ expanded its cyber espionage capabilities to monitor digital communications, intercept internet traffic, and conduct offensive cyber operations against adversaries.

3. **Central Intelligence Agency (CIA):** The CIA, America's premier intelligence agency, has a long history of conducting covert operations and espionage activities around the world. Founded in 1947, the CIA played a pivotal role in gathering intelligence, conducting covert operations, and influencing foreign governments during the Cold War era. In the digital age, the CIA expanded its cyber espionage capabilities to collect intelligence from digital sources, infiltrate enemy networks, and disrupt adversary operations using cyber weapons and techniques.

4. **KGB and GRU:** The KGB, the Soviet Union's main security agency, and the GRU, its military intelligence agency, were instrumental in conducting cyber espionage and surveillance operations during the Cold War. With a focus on gathering intelligence, infiltrating enemy organizations, and conducting covert operations, the KGB and GRU employed a wide range of tactics and techniques to monitor adversaries, steal secrets, and manipulate foreign governments. In the digital age, successor agencies to the KGB and GRU, such as the FSB and SVR, continue to conduct cyber espionage and covert operations on behalf of the Russian government.

5. **Mossad:** Mossad, Israel's intelligence agency, has been a pioneer in cyber espionage and covert operations since its establishment in 1949. With a focus on gathering intelligence, conducting counterterrorism operations, and protecting Israeli interests, Mossad has developed sophisticated cyber espionage capabilities to monitor adversaries, infiltrate enemy networks, and disrupt hostile activities. Mossad's cyber operations have targeted terrorist organizations, rogue states, and adversaries in the Middle East and beyond.

6. **Stuxnet:** Stuxnet, a sophisticated cyber weapon discovered in 2010, was one of the first known instances of a state-sponsored cyber attack targeting industrial control systems. Believed to be developed by the United States and Israel, Stuxnet was designed to sabotage Iran's nuclear program by targeting centrifuge machines used for uranium enrichment. The deployment of Stuxnet marked a significant escalation in cyber warfare tactics and highlighted the potential of cyber weapons to disrupt critical infrastructure and sabotage enemy operations.

7. **Edward Snowden:** Edward Snowden, a former contractor for the NSA, became a whistleblower in 2013 when he leaked classified documents revealing the extent of the NSA's global surveillance programs. Snowden's revelations exposed widespread mass surveillance of internet communications, phone metadata collection, and other intrusive surveillance practices conducted by the NSA and its allies. Snowden's disclosures sparked a global debate on privacy, civil liberties, and government surveillance, leading to calls for greater transparency, accountability, and reform of intelligence agencies' surveillance practices.

8. **Shadow Brokers:** The Shadow Brokers, a mysterious hacking group, gained notoriety in 2016 when they leaked a trove of classified NSA hacking tools and exploits on the dark web. The

leaked tools, which included zero-day vulnerabilities, malware implants, and exploit kits, were allegedly stolen from the NSA's elite hacking unit, the Tailored Access Operations (TAO). The Shadow Brokers' disclosures exposed the vulnerabilities of government cyber weapons and raised concerns about the proliferation of cyber weapons in the hands of malicious actors.

Pioneers of cyber espionage have played pivotal roles in shaping the landscape of intelligence gathering and surveillance in the digital age. From government intelligence agencies to whistleblowers and hacking groups, these individuals and organizations have driven innovation, exposed vulnerabilities, and influenced the evolution of cyber espionage tactics and strategies. By understanding their contributions and motivations, we can gain valuable insights into the complex and evolving nature of cyber espionage in the modern world.

Chapter 3
Becoming a Master Spy in the Digital World

In the digital age, the art of espionage has evolved to encompass a wide array of sophisticated techniques and strategies tailored to exploit the vulnerabilities of the interconnected world. Becoming a master spy in the digital world requires a deep understanding of technology, psychology, and tradecraft, as well as the ability to adapt to rapidly changing threats and environments.

In this chapter, we explore the skills, tactics, and mindset necessary to excel in the field of cyber espionage. From reconnaissance and social engineering to encryption and evasion techniques, mastering the tools of the trade is essential for success in the world of digital espionage. We also delve into the ethical and legal considerations surrounding cyber spying, examining the boundaries of acceptable conduct and the consequences of crossing them.

Whether you aspire to work in intelligence agencies, defend against cyber threats, or simply gain a better understanding of the digital landscape, this chapter will provide valuable insights into the world of cyber espionage and the skills required to navigate it effectively. Join us as we embark on a journey into the clandestine world of digital espionage and uncover the secrets of becoming a master spy in the digital age.

Skills Needed for Cyber Spying

Cyber spying, also known as cyber espionage, is a complex and multifaceted endeavor that requires a diverse set of skills and competencies. From technical expertise to social engineering prowess, cyber spies must possess a wide range of abilities to successfully gather intelligence, infiltrate target networks, and evade detection. In this section, we'll explore the key skills needed for cyber spying and how they contribute to the success of espionage operations.

1. **Technical Proficiency:** Perhaps the most fundamental skill for cyber spies is technical proficiency in various aspects of information technology and cybersecurity. This includes knowledge of computer networks, operating systems, programming languages, and cybersecurity tools. Cyber spies must be adept at navigating complex digital environments, understanding how systems and networks operate, and exploiting vulnerabilities to gain unauthorized access. Proficiency in hacking techniques, malware analysis, and digital forensics is also essential for conducting successful cyber espionage operations.

2. **Social Engineering:** Social engineering is another critical skill for cyber spies, as it involves manipulating individuals or organizations into divulging confidential information, granting access to sensitive systems, or performing actions that benefit the attacker. Social engineering techniques may include phishing, pretexting, baiting, and tailgating, among others. Cyber spies must be skilled at understanding human psychology, building rapport with targets, and crafting persuasive messages or scenarios to elicit desired responses. Effective social engineering can bypass technical defenses and provide cyber spies with valuable access to target networks or information.

3. **Digital Reconnaissance:** Digital reconnaissance, also known as information gathering or intelligence gathering, is the process of collecting and analyzing information about target individuals, organizations, or systems to support espionage operations. Cyber spies must be proficient in conducting open-source intelligence (OSINT) research, scanning networks, analyzing vulnerabilities, and identifying potential targets. Digital reconnaissance provides valuable insights into target behaviors, preferences, and vulnerabilities, enabling cyber spies to tailor their tactics and strategies for maximum impact.

4. **Operational Security (OPSEC):** Operational security, or OPSEC, is the practice of protecting sensitive information and maintaining operational security to prevent adversaries from detecting, intercepting, or disrupting espionage activities. Cyber spies must be skilled at maintaining anonymity, covering their tracks, and avoiding detection by adversaries, security tools, and monitoring systems. This may involve using encryption, anonymization tools, virtual private networks (VPNs), and other counter-surveillance techniques to conceal their identities and activities. Effective OPSEC is crucial for maintaining the secrecy and integrity of espionage operations and protecting the safety of operatives.

5. **Adaptability and Creativity:** Cyber spies must be adaptable and creative in their approach to espionage, as they often face rapidly changing threats, environments, and technologies. The ability to think outside the box, innovate new techniques, and adapt to evolving challenges is essential for staying ahead of adversaries and achieving mission objectives. Cyber spies must constantly update their skills, learn new technologies, and anticipate emerging threats to remain effective in the dynamic world of cyber espionage.

6. **Cultural and Linguistic Skills:** In many cases, cyber spies may need to operate in foreign environments or target individuals from different cultural backgrounds. Cultural and linguistic skills are therefore valuable assets for cyber spies, enabling them to navigate social norms, customs, and language barriers effectively. Proficiency in foreign languages, cultural awareness, and interpersonal communication skills can help cyber spies build rapport with targets, gather intelligence discreetly, and avoid suspicion.

7. **Ethical Awareness:** Ethical awareness is an important consideration for cyber spies, as their actions may have significant ethical, legal, and moral implications. Cyber spies must carefully consider the potential consequences of their actions, adhere to ethical guidelines and legal frameworks, and prioritize the protection of innocent individuals and non-combatants. Upholding ethical standards and conducting espionage with integrity and professionalism is essential for maintaining public trust, preserving national security interests, and avoiding reputational damage.

Cyber spying requires a diverse set of skills and competencies, ranging from technical proficiency to social engineering prowess, adaptability, and ethical awareness. Cyber spies must be adept at navigating complex digital environments, manipulating human behavior, and maintaining operational security to achieve their objectives discreetly and effectively. By mastering these skills and adhering to ethical principles, cyber spies can contribute to national security, gather valuable intelligence, and protect against emerging cyber threats in an increasingly interconnected world.

Training and Recruitment

Training and recruitment are critical aspects of building a skilled workforce for cyber espionage and intelligence gathering operations.

As the digital landscape continues to evolve and cyber threats become more sophisticated, governments, intelligence agencies, and private organizations invest in training programs and recruitment initiatives to identify, develop, and deploy talented individuals with the skills and expertise needed to conduct effective cyber spying operations. In this section, we'll explore the key elements of training and recruitment for cyber espionage and intelligence gathering.

1. **Identifying Talent:** The first step in building a skilled workforce for cyber espionage is identifying individuals with the aptitude, skills, and potential to excel in this field. Recruitment efforts may target individuals with backgrounds in computer science, cybersecurity, engineering, mathematics, or related fields, as well as those with experience in military, law enforcement, or intelligence agencies. Recruiters may look for candidates who demonstrate technical proficiency, problem-solving abilities, analytical skills, creativity, and adaptability, as well as a strong sense of ethics, integrity, and discretion.

2. **Recruitment Initiatives:** Intelligence agencies and government organizations often conduct targeted recruitment initiatives to attract talent for cyber espionage and intelligence gathering operations. These initiatives may include job fairs, recruitment events, internship programs, scholarship opportunities, and outreach efforts to engage with students, professionals, and experts in the cybersecurity community. Recruiters may also leverage social media, professional networks, and specialized websites to identify and connect with potential candidates who possess the desired skills and qualifications.

3. **Security Clearance:** Due to the sensitive nature of cyber espionage operations, candidates for roles in intelligence agencies and government organizations must undergo thorough background checks and obtain security clearances before they

can access classified information or participate in espionage activities. Security clearance processes typically involve background investigations, interviews, polygraph tests, and evaluations of an individual's loyalty, trustworthiness, and suitability for handling classified information. Clearance levels may vary depending on the sensitivity of the information and the nature of the espionage operations involved.

4. **Technical Training:** Once recruited, cyber spies undergo specialized technical training to develop the skills and expertise needed to conduct effective cyber espionage operations. Training programs may cover a wide range of topics, including computer networks, operating systems, programming languages, cybersecurity tools, hacking techniques, digital forensics, and encryption methods. Hands-on exercises, simulations, and real-world scenarios may be used to reinforce learning and provide practical experience in conducting espionage operations.

5. **Social Engineering Skills:** In addition to technical training, cyber spies receive training in social engineering techniques to manipulate individuals or organizations into divulging confidential information, granting access to sensitive systems, or performing actions that benefit the attacker. Training programs may cover topics such as phishing, pretexting, baiting, tailgating, and psychological manipulation, as well as interpersonal communication skills, rapport-building techniques, and cultural awareness. Role-playing exercises and simulations may be used to practice social engineering tactics in realistic scenarios.

6. **Operational Security (OPSEC):** Operational security, or OPSEC, is an essential component of training for cyber spies, as it involves protecting sensitive information and maintaining operational security to prevent adversaries from detecting, intercepting, or disrupting espionage activities. Training programs may cover topics such as anonymity, encryption,

counter-surveillance techniques, and best practices for maintaining operational security in digital environments. Cyber spies learn how to cover their tracks, avoid detection by adversaries, and protect the secrecy and integrity of espionage operations.

7. **Ethical and Legal Considerations:** Cyber spies receive training in ethical and legal considerations surrounding espionage activities, including the boundaries of acceptable conduct, the consequences of violating laws or regulations, and the potential ethical dilemmas they may encounter in the course of their work. Training programs emphasize the importance of upholding ethical standards, respecting privacy rights, and adhering to legal frameworks governing intelligence gathering and surveillance operations. Cyber spies are trained to conduct espionage with integrity, professionalism, and respect for human rights, while prioritizing the protection of innocent individuals and non-combatants.

8. **Continuing Education and Professional Development:** Cyber spies engage in continuing education and professional development to stay abreast of emerging technologies, evolving threats, and best practices in cyber espionage and intelligence gathering. Training programs may include ongoing coursework, seminars, workshops, conferences, and certifications to enhance skills, expand knowledge, and keep operatives up-to-date with the latest developments in the field. Continuous learning and professional development are essential for maintaining operational effectiveness, adapting to changing environments, and mitigating emerging threats in the dynamic world of cyber espionage.

Training and recruitment are critical components of building a skilled workforce for cyber espionage and intelligence gathering operations. By identifying talent, conducting targeted recruitment initiatives, providing specialized training, and emphasizing ethical and legal considerations, intelligence agencies and government organizations can develop a cadre of highly trained cyber spies capable of conducting effective espionage operations in the digital age. Continued investment in training and recruitment efforts is essential for maintaining national security, protecting against cyber threats, and safeguarding the interests of nations and their citizens in an increasingly interconnected world.

The Rise of Digital Masterminds

The digital age has ushered in a new era of espionage, characterized by the use of advanced technologies, sophisticated tactics, and covert operations conducted in cyberspace. As the world becomes increasingly interconnected and reliant on digital technologies, the opportunities for cyber espionage have expanded dramatically, allowing skilled operatives known as "digital masterminds" to wield unprecedented power and influence in the clandestine world of intelligence gathering. In this chapter, we explore the rise of digital masterminds and their impact on the evolution of cyber espionage in the modern era.

1. **The Digital Revolution:** The digital revolution, marked by the proliferation of personal computers, the internet, and digital communication networks, has transformed the landscape of espionage and intelligence gathering. With the advent of cyberspace, intelligence agencies and governments gained new opportunities to gather intelligence, conduct surveillance, and influence foreign adversaries without the need for physical presence or direct confrontation. The digital revolution democratized access to information, allowing skilled operatives to leverage technology to collect, analyze, and exploit vast amounts of data for espionage purposes.

2. **Skills and Expertise:** Digital masterminds possess a unique combination of technical skills, strategic thinking, and creativity that sets them apart from traditional spies. These operatives are highly proficient in computer networks, cybersecurity, cryptography, hacking techniques, and digital forensics, allowing them to navigate complex digital environments, exploit vulnerabilities, and bypass security measures with ease. Digital masterminds are also adept at social engineering, manipulation, and psychological warfare, enabling them to manipulate individuals, organizations, and systems to achieve their objectives.

3. **Adversarial Tactics:** Digital masterminds employ a wide range of adversarial tactics and techniques to conduct cyber espionage operations against their adversaries. These tactics may include phishing attacks, malware infections, social engineering schemes, and supply chain compromises, among others. Digital masterminds leverage sophisticated tools and technologies to infiltrate target networks, exfiltrate sensitive information, and maintain persistent access to compromised systems. By exploiting vulnerabilities in software, hardware, and human behavior, digital masterminds can penetrate even the most secure environments and evade detection for extended periods.

4. **Nation-State Actors:** Nation-state actors, including intelligence agencies and government-sponsored hacking groups, are among the most prolific users of digital masterminds for cyber espionage purposes. These actors conduct espionage operations to gather intelligence, monitor adversaries, disrupt enemy activities, and advance national security interests in cyberspace. Nation-state actors often operate with substantial resources, advanced capabilities, and strategic objectives that enable them to conduct sophisticated and highly targeted cyber espionage

campaigns against foreign governments, military organizations, critical infrastructure, and private sector entities.

5. **Non-State Actors:** Non-state actors, such as hacktivist groups, cybercriminal organizations, and terrorist networks, also employ digital masterminds to conduct cyber espionage operations for political, financial, or ideological reasons. These actors may target government agencies, corporations, media organizations, or individuals to steal sensitive information, disrupt operations, or spread propaganda in support of their goals. Non-state actors often operate with greater agility, flexibility, and anonymity than nation-state actors, making them difficult to detect and attribute in cyberspace.

6. **Private Sector Entities:** Private sector entities, including corporations, research institutions, and cybersecurity firms, also employ digital masterminds to conduct espionage operations for competitive advantage, intellectual property theft, or corporate espionage purposes. These actors may engage in industrial espionage, economic espionage, or insider threat activities to gain access to proprietary information, trade secrets, or sensitive data belonging to competitors, partners, or clients. Private sector digital masterminds may operate with greater discretion and sophistication than their counterparts in the public sector, leveraging insider knowledge, trusted relationships, and access to privileged information to achieve their objectives.

7. **Global Implications:** The rise of digital masterminds has profound global implications for security, diplomacy, and geopolitics in the 21st century. Cyber espionage operations conducted by nation-state actors, non-state actors, and private sector entities can have far-reaching consequences, including political destabilization, economic disruption, and social unrest. The attribution of cyber attacks and espionage operations is often challenging due to the anonymity, deniability, and

deception tactics employed by digital masterminds, leading to tensions between nations, mistrust among allies, and escalating cyber conflicts.

8. **Countermeasures and Defenses:** Governments, organizations, and individuals must deploy robust countermeasures and defenses to mitigate the threats posed by digital masterminds and cyber espionage operations. This includes investing in cybersecurity infrastructure, implementing best practices for network security, conducting regular risk assessments and vulnerability assessments, and educating users about the risks of social engineering and phishing attacks. Collaboration between governments, international organizations, and the private sector is essential for sharing threat intelligence, coordinating responses, and developing collective defenses against cyber espionage threats.

The rise of digital masterminds has transformed the landscape of cyber espionage, ushering in a new era of intelligence gathering and surveillance in the digital age. These skilled operatives leverage advanced technologies, sophisticated tactics, and adversarial techniques to conduct espionage operations against adversaries in cyberspace. As the world becomes increasingly interconnected and reliant on digital technologies, the importance of understanding, detecting, and mitigating the threats posed by digital masterminds cannot be overstated. By investing in cybersecurity, enhancing threat intelligence capabilities, and fostering collaboration between governments, organizations, and the private sector, we can collectively defend against cyber espionage threats and safeguard the integrity, security, and stability of cyberspace for future generations.

Chapter 4
Tools Cyber Spies Use

In the clandestine world of cyber espionage, operatives rely on a diverse array of tools and technologies to conduct surveillance, gather intelligence, and infiltrate target networks. These tools, ranging from sophisticated malware and hacking utilities to encryption software and covert communication channels, empower cyber spies to navigate the complexities of cyberspace and achieve their objectives discreetly and effectively. In this chapter, we delve into the arsenal of tools cyber spies use, exploring their capabilities, applications, and implications for intelligence gathering and surveillance operations.

As the digital landscape continues to evolve and cyber threats become more sophisticated, understanding the tools cyber spies use is essential for identifying, detecting, and mitigating espionage activities. From reconnaissance and exploitation tools to communication and exfiltration utilities, each tool serves a specific purpose in the cyber espionage toolkit, enabling operatives to conduct covert operations, evade detection, and maintain operational security in the digital realm. By examining the tools cyber spies use, we can gain valuable insights into their tactics, techniques, and procedures, as well as the evolving nature of cyber espionage in the modern era.

Malware and Viruses

Malware and viruses represent some of the most potent weapons in the arsenal of cyber spies. These malicious software programs are designed to infiltrate computer systems, compromise data, and enable unauthorized access to sensitive information. In the realm of cyber espionage, malware and viruses play a crucial role in facilitating surveillance, gathering intelligence, and conducting covert operations against adversaries. In this section, we'll explore in detail the nature of malware and viruses, their characteristics, capabilities, and the implications for cybersecurity in the digital age.

1. **Understanding Malware:**

Malware, short for malicious software, refers to a broad category of software programs specifically designed to infiltrate, damage, or compromise computer systems, networks, or devices. Malware encompasses a wide range of malicious programs, including viruses, worms, Trojans, ransomware, spyware, adware, and rootkits, each with its own distinct characteristics and functionalities. Malware is typically deployed by cybercriminals, hackers, or state-sponsored actors for various malicious purposes, including data theft, financial fraud, espionage, sabotage, and extortion.

2. **Types of Malware:**

   a) **Viruses:** Viruses are malicious programs that attach themselves to legitimate files or programs and replicate themselves to spread to other systems. Once activated, viruses can execute malicious code, steal data, corrupt files, or disrupt system operations.

   b) **Worms:** Worms are self-replicating malware programs that spread across computer networks by exploiting vulnerabilities in software or exploiting weak passwords. Worms can propagate rapidly and infect large numbers of devices, causing widespread damage or disruption.

   c) **Trojans:** Trojans, named after the legendary Greek horse, disguise themselves as legitimate programs or files to trick users into downloading and executing them. Once installed, Trojans can perform various malicious actions, such as stealing sensitive information, spying on user activities, or providing remote access to attackers.

d) **Ransomware:** Ransomware is a type of malware that encrypts files or locks down computer systems, rendering them inaccessible to users. Attackers demand a ransom payment in exchange for decrypting the files or restoring access to the system. Ransomware attacks can have devastating consequences for individuals, businesses, and organizations, causing data loss, financial loss, and reputational damage.

e) **Spyware:** Spyware is a type of malware designed to secretly monitor and collect information about a user's activities, such as browsing habits, keystrokes, and personal information. Spyware can be used for espionage, identity theft, or targeted advertising purposes.

f) **Adware:** Adware is a type of malware that displays unwanted advertisements or redirects users to malicious websites. Adware can slow down system performance, consume bandwidth, and compromise user privacy by tracking browsing activities.

g) **Rootkits:** Rootkits are stealthy malware programs that conceal their presence on infected systems by subverting or disabling security mechanisms. Rootkits can provide attackers with privileged access to system resources, allowing them to execute malicious code, steal sensitive information, or maintain persistent control over compromised systems.

3. **Distribution and Infection Vectors:**

Malware can be distributed through various infection vectors, including:

   a) **Email Attachments:** Malware-laden email attachments, such as executable files, documents, or scripts, are a common infection vector used by cybercriminals to distribute malware to unsuspecting users.

   b) **Phishing Links:** Phishing emails containing malicious links or URLs can lead users to websites hosting malware or exploit kits designed to infect their systems.

   c) **Drive-by Downloads:** Drive-by downloads occur when users inadvertently download malware by visiting compromised or malicious websites that exploit vulnerabilities in their web browsers or plugins.

   d) **Removable Media:** Malware can spread through removable media, such as USB drives or external hard drives, when infected devices are connected to vulnerable systems.

   e) **Exploit Kits:** Exploit kits are malicious toolkits used to exploit vulnerabilities in software or operating systems to deliver malware payloads to unsuspecting users.

4. **Capabilities and Functionality:**

Malware can possess a wide range of capabilities and functionalities, depending on the specific type and purpose of the malicious program. Some common capabilities of malware include:

   a) **Remote Access:** Malware can provide attackers with remote access to compromised systems, allowing them to execute commands, exfiltrate data, or install additional malware.

b) **Data Theft:** Malware can steal sensitive information, such as login credentials, financial data, or personal information, from infected systems and transmit it to remote servers controlled by attackers.

c) **System Modification:** Malware can modify system settings, registry entries, or configuration files to maintain persistence, evade detection, or disable security mechanisms.

d) **Distributed Denial-of-Service (DDoS):** Some types of malware, such as botnets, can be used to launch DDoS attacks by coordinating large numbers of infected devices to flood target servers or networks with malicious traffic, causing service disruptions or outages.

e) **Encryption and Ransomware:** Ransomware malware encrypts files or locks down systems, rendering them inaccessible to users until a ransom payment is made to the attackers.

5. Detection and Mitigation:

Detecting and mitigating malware threats requires a multi-layered approach to cybersecurity that includes:

a) **Antivirus Software:** Antivirus software can detect and remove known malware signatures from infected systems by scanning files, processes, and network traffic for malicious activity.

b) **Intrusion Detection Systems (IDS):** IDS solutions monitor network traffic for suspicious behavior or patterns indicative of malware infections, unauthorized access attempts, or other security threats.

c) **Firewalls:** Firewalls can block malicious traffic and prevent unauthorized access to network resources by filtering incoming and outgoing network traffic based on predefined security rules.

d) **Security Updates and Patches:** Regularly applying security updates and patches to software, operating systems, and firmware can help mitigate vulnerabilities that could be exploited by malware.

e) **User Education and Awareness:** Educating users about the risks of malware, phishing, and other cyber threats can help prevent infections by encouraging safe browsing habits, cautious email behavior, and adherence to security best practices.

6. Emerging Threats and Future Trends:

As technology continues to evolve, malware authors are constantly innovating new techniques and strategies to evade detection, exploit vulnerabilities, and infect target systems. Some emerging trends and future threats in the field of malware include:

a) **Fileless Malware:** Fileless malware attacks leverage memory-based techniques to execute malicious code without leaving traces on disk, making them difficult to detect using traditional antivirus solutions.

b) **Polymorphic Malware:** Polymorphic malware variants use advanced obfuscation techniques to dynamically change their code and behavior, making them resistant to signature-based detection methods.

c) **IoT Malware:** Malware targeting Internet of Things (IoT) devices, such as smart home devices, industrial control systems, and medical devices, poses new security challenges due to the proliferation of insecure and vulnerable IoT devices connected to the internet.

d) **AI-Powered Malware:** Malware authors may leverage artificial intelligence (AI) and machine learning (ML) techniques to develop more sophisticated and adaptive malware variants capable of evading detection and bypassing security defenses.

e) **Supply Chain Attacks:** Supply chain attacks target software vendors, suppliers, or third-party service providers to compromise their products or services and distribute malware to unsuspecting customers or users.

Malware and viruses represent formidable threats to cybersecurity in the digital age, capable of infiltrating systems, compromising data, and enabling unauthorized access to sensitive information. Understanding the nature of malware, its distribution methods, capabilities, and detection techniques is essential for mitigating the risks posed by cyber threats and safeguarding the integrity, security, and privacy of computer systems and networks. By implementing robust security measures, raising awareness among users, and staying vigilant against emerging threats, organizations and individuals can effectively defend against malware attacks and protect against the evolving challenges of cyber espionage in the modern era.

Hacking Techniques

Hacking techniques encompass a diverse set of skills, tools, and methodologies used by individuals or groups to gain unauthorized access to computer systems, networks, or data. While hacking techniques can be employed for various purposes, including security testing, research, and ethical hacking, they are often associated with malicious activities such as cyber espionage, data breaches, and cybercrime. In this section, we'll explore some of the most common hacking techniques used by cybercriminals, hackers, and state-sponsored actors to compromise systems and exploit vulnerabilities.

1. **Phishing:** Phishing is a social engineering technique used to trick individuals into divulging sensitive information, such as login credentials, credit card numbers, or personal data, by masquerading as a trustworthy entity in electronic communications. Phishing attacks typically involve fraudulent emails, text messages, or websites that impersonate legitimate organizations, such as banks, social media platforms, or government agencies, and prompt recipients to click on malicious links, download malware-infected attachments, or enter their confidential information into spoofed login forms.

2. **Exploiting Software Vulnerabilities:** Software vulnerabilities, such as programming errors, design flaws, or misconfigurations, can be exploited by hackers to gain unauthorized access to systems or execute arbitrary code. Common types of software vulnerabilities include buffer overflows, SQL injection, cross-site scripting (XSS), and remote code execution (RCE). Hackers often use automated tools, such as vulnerability scanners or exploit kits, to identify and exploit known vulnerabilities in software, operating systems, or web applications.

3. **Brute Force Attacks:** Brute force attacks involve systematically trying every possible combination of characters until the correct password or encryption key is discovered. Brute force attacks are commonly used to crack passwords, gain unauthorized access to user accounts, or decrypt encrypted data. Hackers may use specialized software or scripts to automate the brute force attack process and increase their chances of success, especially against weak or poorly chosen passwords.

4. **Social Engineering:** Social engineering techniques exploit human psychology and manipulate individuals into performing actions or divulging sensitive information that can be used to compromise security. Social engineering attacks may involve impersonating trusted individuals or authority figures, such as IT administrators, coworkers, or customer support representatives, to gain the trust of victims and deceive them into revealing confidential information, granting access to restricted areas, or executing malicious actions on their behalf.

5. **Man-in-the-Middle (MITM) Attacks:** Man-in-the-middle attacks intercept communication between two parties, such as a user and a website or two devices communicating over a network, and eavesdrop on or modify the data exchanged between them. MITM attacks can be used to steal sensitive information, such as login credentials or financial data, hijack sessions, inject malicious code into web pages, or impersonate legitimate websites or services to deceive users.

6. **SQL Injection (SQLi):** SQL injection attacks exploit vulnerabilities in web applications that use SQL databases by inserting malicious SQL queries into input fields or parameters. SQL injection attacks can manipulate database queries, extract sensitive information from databases, or execute arbitrary commands on the underlying database server. SQL injection attacks are commonly used to steal user credentials, deface websites, or compromise sensitive data stored in databases.

7. **Cross-Site Scripting (XSS):** Cross-site scripting attacks inject malicious scripts into web pages viewed by other users, such as visitors to a compromised website or users of a vulnerable web application. XSS attacks can steal session cookies, hijack user sessions, redirect users to malicious websites, or deface web pages. Hackers may use reflected XSS, stored XSS, or DOM-based XSS techniques to execute malicious scripts in the context

of a victim's browser and exploit vulnerabilities in web applications.

8. **Remote Code Execution (RCE):** Remote code execution vulnerabilities allow hackers to execute arbitrary code on a target system or application remotely, without authentication or user interaction. RCE vulnerabilities are often found in web servers, web applications, or network services that fail to properly validate input or sanitize user-supplied data. Hackers can exploit RCE vulnerabilities to gain unauthorized access to systems, install malware, or take control of compromised devices.

Hacking techniques represent a significant threat to cybersecurity, as they can be used by malicious actors to exploit vulnerabilities, compromise systems, and steal sensitive information. Understanding the nature of hacking techniques, their methodologies, and the risks they pose is essential for implementing effective security measures, conducting security assessments, and mitigating the risks of cyber attacks. By staying informed about emerging threats, adopting best practices for cybersecurity, and investing in robust security controls, organizations and individuals can defend against hacking techniques and protect against the evolving challenges of cybercrime and cyber espionage in the digital age.

Surveillance Technology

Surveillance technology encompasses a broad range of tools, techniques, and systems used to monitor, record, and analyze activities, behaviors, or communications of individuals or groups for various purposes, including law enforcement, security, intelligence gathering, and public safety. From closed-circuit television (CCTV) cameras and facial recognition systems to satellite imagery and internet monitoring tools, surveillance technology plays a critical role in modern society, shaping how information is collected, processed, and utilized for monitoring and control purposes. In this section, we'll explore in detail the nature of surveillance technology, its capabilities, applications, and the implications for privacy, civil liberties, and security in the digital age.

1. Closed-Circuit Television (CCTV) Cameras:

Closed-circuit television (CCTV) cameras are widely used for video surveillance in public spaces, such as streets, parks, airports, train stations, and shopping malls, as well as private properties, businesses, and government facilities. CCTV cameras capture live video footage of people, vehicles, and activities in real-time, providing valuable situational awareness and forensic evidence for law enforcement, security personnel, and investigators. Modern CCTV systems may include features such as high-definition video recording, remote monitoring, motion detection, and facial recognition capabilities to enhance their effectiveness and functionality.

2. Facial Recognition Systems:

Facial recognition systems use biometric technology to identify or verify individuals based on their unique facial features, such as the size, shape, and arrangement of facial landmarks (e.g., eyes, nose, mouth). Facial recognition algorithms analyze live or recorded video footage to detect and match faces against a database of known individuals or watchlists, enabling real-time identification and tracking of persons of interest. Facial recognition systems are used in various applications, including law enforcement, border control, airport security, access control, and surveillance, but they raise concerns about privacy, accuracy, bias, and civil liberties due to their potential for mass surveillance and misuse.

3. License Plate Recognition (LPR) Systems:

License plate recognition (LPR) systems, also known as automatic license plate recognition (ALPR) systems, use optical character recognition (OCR) technology to capture, read, and record license plate numbers from vehicles passing through a monitored area. LPR systems can be deployed on stationary cameras mounted at fixed locations, such as toll booths, parking lots, or traffic intersections, or on mobile platforms, such as police patrol cars or surveillance drones, to collect vehicle data for law enforcement, traffic management, parking enforcement, or surveillance purposes. LPR systems can provide real-time alerts for stolen vehicles, wanted suspects, or vehicles of interest, but they also raise concerns about privacy, data retention, and surveillance without consent.

4. GPS Tracking and Location-Based Services:

Global Positioning System (GPS) tracking technology uses satellite signals to determine the precise location, speed, and direction of vehicles, objects, or individuals equipped with GPS-enabled devices, such as smartphones, tablets, or vehicle navigation systems. GPS tracking systems can be used for fleet management, asset tracking, personal navigation, and location-based services, but they also raise concerns about privacy, surveillance, and tracking without consent. Law enforcement agencies may use GPS tracking devices or cell phone location data to monitor the movements of suspects, gather evidence, or conduct surveillance operations, subject to legal restrictions and oversight.

5. Internet and Communications Monitoring:

Internet and communications monitoring technologies are used to intercept, capture, and analyze electronic communications, such as emails, phone calls, text messages, or internet browsing activity, for surveillance, intelligence gathering, or law enforcement purposes. Surveillance technologies may include network monitoring tools, packet sniffers, wiretapping devices, or data interception systems deployed by government agencies, law enforcement, or intelligence services to monitor communications networks, collect metadata, or intercept content in transit. Internet and communications monitoring raise concerns about privacy, freedom of expression, and civil liberties, as they can enable mass surveillance, censorship, or unwarranted intrusion into private communications.

6. Biometric Identification and Authentication:

Biometric identification and authentication technologies use unique physiological or behavioral characteristics, such as fingerprints, iris patterns, voiceprints, or DNA profiles, to verify the identity of individuals or grant access to secured areas, devices, or systems. Biometric systems may include fingerprint scanners, iris scanners, facial recognition systems, voice recognition software, or DNA analysis tools used in various applications, including border control, access control, authentication, and surveillance. Biometric technologies offer advantages in terms of accuracy, convenience, and security, but they also raise concerns about privacy, data protection, and the risk of biometric data breaches or misuse.

7. Satellite Imaging and Remote Sensing:

Satellite imaging and remote sensing technologies use satellite-based sensors and cameras to capture high-resolution imagery and data of the Earth's surface, atmosphere, or oceans for various applications, including environmental monitoring, agriculture, urban planning, disaster management, and surveillance. Satellite imagery can provide real-time or historical data on land use, vegetation cover, natural disasters, infrastructure development, or military activities, enabling governments, researchers, and organizations to analyze trends, detect anomalies, and monitor changes over time. Satellite imaging and remote sensing raise concerns about privacy, surveillance, and the potential for mass surveillance or reconnaissance capabilities in the hands of governments or intelligence agencies.

8. Social Media Monitoring and Data Analytics:

Social media monitoring and data analytics technologies analyze publicly available data from social media platforms, such as Facebook, Twitter, Instagram, or LinkedIn, to gather insights, track trends, or monitor public sentiment on specific topics, events, or individuals. Social media monitoring tools may use keyword searches, sentiment analysis, or network analysis techniques to identify influencers, detect emerging threats, or track the spread of misinformation or propaganda campaigns. Social media monitoring raises concerns about privacy, data protection, and the potential for surveillance, censorship, or manipulation of public discourse by governments, corporations, or political actors.

Surveillance technology plays a significant role in modern society, shaping how information is collected, processed, and utilized for monitoring and control purposes. While surveillance technology offers benefits in terms of security, public safety, and intelligence gathering, it also raises concerns about privacy, civil liberties, and the potential for abuse or misuse by governments, corporations, or malicious actors. Balancing the benefits and risks of surveillance technology requires careful consideration of ethical, legal, and regulatory frameworks to safeguard individual rights, protect personal data, and ensure accountability, transparency, and oversight in the use of surveillance technologies in the digital age.

Chapter 5
Types of Cyber Spies

Cyber espionage is a multifaceted and dynamic field, with various actors operating at different levels of sophistication and intent. In this chapter, we delve into the diverse landscape of cyber spies, exploring the different types of actors, their motivations, tactics, and the impact they have on cybersecurity and national security. From nation-state actors conducting strategic intelligence operations to cybercriminal organizations seeking financial gain, and from hacktivist groups promoting political or ideological agendas to insider threats exploiting internal vulnerabilities, the world of cyber espionage is populated by a wide range of adversaries with distinct characteristics and objectives. By understanding the types of cyber spies and their modus operandi, organizations and governments can better prepare for and mitigate the threats posed by cyber espionage in the digital age.

State-Sponsored Spies

State-sponsored spies, also known as state-sponsored hackers or advanced persistent threats (APTs), represent one of the most formidable and sophisticated categories of cyber spies operating in the digital landscape. These operatives are sponsored, directed, or supported by nation-states to conduct intelligence gathering, surveillance, sabotage, or cyber warfare operations against foreign governments, military organizations, critical infrastructure, corporations, or individuals. State-sponsored spies leverage advanced technologies, sophisticated tactics, and significant resources to achieve their strategic objectives, which may include stealing sensitive information, disrupting adversary activities, or advancing national security interests. In this section, we'll explore in detail the nature of state-sponsored spies, their motivations, tactics, and the implications for cybersecurity and geopolitics in the modern era.

1. **Motivations and Objectives:**

State-sponsored spies are motivated by a range of political, economic, military, or strategic objectives determined by their sponsoring nation-states. Some common motivations for state-sponsored espionage include:

- a) **National Security:** State-sponsored spies may gather intelligence on foreign governments, military capabilities, or defense systems to enhance national security, assess threats, or inform strategic decision-making by policymakers and military leaders.

- b) **Political Influence:** State-sponsored spies may conduct influence operations, propaganda campaigns, or disinformation campaigns to manipulate public opinion, undermine political adversaries, or influence elections in foreign countries.

- c) **Economic Espionage:** State-sponsored spies may steal intellectual property, trade secrets, or proprietary information from foreign corporations or research institutions to gain competitive advantages, promote economic growth, or advance industrial development in their own countries.

- d) **Cyber Warfare:** State-sponsored spies may engage in cyber warfare operations, such as sabotage, disruption, or destruction of critical infrastructure, government networks, or military systems, to achieve strategic objectives, exert influence, or retaliate against adversaries in times of conflict.

2. Tactics and Techniques:

State-sponsored spies employ a wide range of tactics, techniques, and procedures (TTPs) to conduct covert intelligence gathering operations, infiltrate target networks, and evade detection by defenders. Some common tactics and techniques used by state-sponsored spies include:

a) **Targeted Intrusions:** State-sponsored spies conduct targeted intrusions against specific individuals, organizations, or systems of interest using sophisticated malware, spear phishing emails, or zero-day exploits to gain initial access and establish persistent presence in target networks.

b) **Advanced Persistent Threats (APTs):** State-sponsored spies often operate as advanced persistent threats (APTs), employing stealthy, persistent, and sophisticated attack methods to maintain long-term access to compromised systems, exfiltrate sensitive data, or conduct espionage activities without being detected.

c) **Supply Chain Attacks:** State-sponsored spies may target suppliers, contractors, or service providers in the supply chain of targeted organizations to gain access to their networks, systems, or data and infiltrate the primary target through trusted relationships or trusted connections.

d) **Watering Hole Attacks:** State-sponsored spies may compromise websites frequented by targeted individuals or organizations and inject malicious code or malware into web pages to infect visitors' devices, steal credentials, or conduct reconnaissance on target networks.

e) **Zero-Day Exploits:** State-sponsored spies may exploit previously unknown vulnerabilities, known as zero-day exploits, in software, operating systems, or network infrastructure to gain unauthorized access to systems, escalate privileges, or execute arbitrary code without detection.

3. **Attribution Challenges:**

Attributing cyber attacks or espionage operations to specific nation-states or state-sponsored actors is often challenging due to the use of proxy servers, false flag operations, or deception tactics to obfuscate the origins of attacks and mislead investigators. State-sponsored spies may employ techniques such as routing attacks through multiple countries, using compromised infrastructure, or employing malware with built-in countermeasures to conceal their identities and evade detection by forensic analysts, incident responders, or intelligence agencies.

4. **Notable Examples:**

   a) **APT28 (Fancy Bear):** APT28, also known as Fancy Bear, is believed to be a Russian state-sponsored cyber espionage group associated with the Russian military intelligence agency GRU. APT28 has been implicated in a wide range of cyber attacks, including the 2016 Democratic National Committee (DNC) email hack, the 2017 French presidential election hack, and various cyber espionage campaigns targeting governments, military organizations, and critical infrastructure sectors worldwide.

   b) **APT29 (Cozy Bear):** APT29, also known as Cozy Bear, is believed to be another Russian state-sponsored cyber espionage group associated with the Russian Federal Security Service (FSB). APT29 has been linked to various cyber attacks, including the 2014 breach of the US State Department email system, the 2015 breach of the White House email system, and the 2016 breach of the Democratic National Committee (DNC) email system.

   c) **APT1 (Comment Crew):** APT1, also known as Comment Crew, is believed to be a Chinese state-sponsored cyber espionage group associated with the People's Liberation Army (PLA) Unit 61398. APT1 has been implicated in numerous cyber attacks targeting governments, military organizations, defense contractors and technology companies worldwide, with a focus on stealing intellectual property, trade secrets, and proprietary information for economic espionage purposes.

5. **Counter measures and Mitigation:**

Defending against state-sponsored spies requires a comprehensive approach to cybersecurity that includes:

   a) **Threat Intelligence:** Organizations should leverage threat intelligence feeds, cybersecurity research reports, and information sharing partnerships to stay informed about emerging threats, TTPs, and indicators of compromise associated with state-sponsored espionage groups.

   b) **Cyber Hygiene:** Organizations should implement basic cybersecurity best practices, such as regular software updates, patch management, network segmentation, access controls, and employee training, to reduce the attack surface and mitigate the risk of compromise by state-sponsored spies.

   c) **Defense-in-Depth:** Organizations should deploy multiple layers of defense, including firewalls, intrusion detection systems (IDS), intrusion prevention systems (IPS), endpoint security solutions, and security monitoring tools, to detect, prevent, and respond to cyber attacks by state-sponsored actors.

d) **Incident Response:** Organizations should develop incident response plans, playbooks, and procedures to quickly detect, contain, and mitigate cyber attacks by state-sponsored spies, minimize damage, and restore normal operations in the event of a security breach.

State-sponsored spies represent a significant and persistent threat to cybersecurity, national security, and global stability, as they leverage advanced technologies, sophisticated tactics, and significant resources to conduct covert intelligence gathering operations, espionage campaigns, or cyber attacks against foreign adversaries. Defending against state-sponsored spies requires a multi-faceted approach that includes threat intelligence, cyber hygiene, defense-in-depth, and incident response capabilities to detect, prevent, and mitigate the risks posed by state-sponsored cyber espionage in the digital age. By understanding the motivations, tactics, and capabilities of state-sponsored spies, organizations and governments can better prepare for and respond to the evolving challenges of cyber warfare and espionage in the modern era.

Hacktivists

Hacktivists represent a unique category of cyber spies who combine hacking skills with political or ideological motivations to promote social change, raise awareness about specific issues, or challenge perceived injustices through cyber attacks, website defacements, data breaches, or online activism. Unlike traditional cyber criminals or state-sponsored spies, hacktivists operate independently or as part of loosely organized groups, such as hacktivist collectives or hacktivist organizations, and often operate under pseudonyms or anonymous identities to evade detection by authorities. In this section, we'll explore in detail the nature of hacktivism, its motivations, tactics, and the implications for cybersecurity, freedom of expression, and civil liberties in the digital age.

1. **Motivations and Objectives:**

Hacktivists are motivated by a range of political, social, or ideological causes, including:

a) **Freedom of Expression:** Hacktivists may seek to defend or promote freedom of expression, speech, or information by targeting governments, corporations, or institutions that censor or restrict access to online content, suppress dissent, or violate human rights.

b) **Social Justice:** Hacktivists may advocate for social justice, equality, or civil rights by exposing corruption, injustice, or abuses of power through data leaks, whistleblowing, or digital protests aimed at raising public awareness and holding perpetrators accountable.

c) **Environmental Activism:** Hacktivists may engage in environmental activism or eco-terrorism by targeting companies or organizations engaged in environmental destruction, pollution, or unsustainable practices through cyber attacks, website defacements, or distributed denial-of-service (DDoS) attacks.

d) **Political Activism:** Hacktivists may support political movements, parties, or causes by disrupting political opponents, leaking sensitive information, or defacing government websites to express dissent, protest government policies, or challenge the status quo.

2. **Tactics and Techniques:**

Hacktivists employ a variety of tactics and techniques to achieve their objectives, including:

a) **Website Defacements:** Hacktivists may deface websites by modifying or replacing the content of web pages with political messages, slogans, or symbols to raise awareness about specific issues, promote their cause, or embarrass their targets.

b) **Data Breaches:** Hacktivists may conduct data breaches or cyber attacks against governments, corporations, or institutions to steal sensitive information, such as confidential documents, emails, or user data, and leak it to the public or media to expose wrongdoing or hold perpetrators accountable.

c) **Distributed Denial-of-Service (DDoS) Attacks:** Hacktivists may launch DDoS attacks against websites, servers, or online services to disrupt operations, render them inaccessible to users, or protest against their activities by flooding them with large volumes of traffic or requests.

d) **Social Media Campaigns:** Hacktivists may use social media platforms, such as Twitter, Facebook, or YouTube, to spread propaganda, share information, coordinate activities, or recruit supporters for their cause through online activism or digital protests.

e) **Cyber Vandalism:** Hacktivists may engage in cyber vandalism by defacing or vandalizing online properties, such as websites, social media accounts, or digital assets, to express dissent, protest, or challenge the legitimacy of their targets.

3. **Notable Examples:**

a) **Anonymous:** Anonymous is a decentralized hacktivist collective known for its cyber attacks, website defacements, and online activism campaigns targeting governments, corporations, and institutions worldwide. Anonymous has been involved in various operations, such as Operation Payback, Operation Tunisia, Operation Egypt, and Operation AntiSec, aimed at promoting freedom of expression, fighting censorship, and supporting political or social causes.

b) **WikiLeaks:** WikiLeaks is a non-profit organization founded by Julian Assange that publishes classified or confidential documents, leaks, and whistleblowing submissions from anonymous sources to expose government secrets, corruption, or human rights abuses. WikiLeaks has released thousands of documents, including diplomatic cables, military records, and corporate emails, revealing sensitive information about governments, intelligence agencies, and corporations worldwide.

c) **LulzSec:** LulzSec, short for Lulz Security, was a hacking group affiliated with Anonymous known for its high-profile cyber attacks, data breaches, and website defacements targeting governments, corporations, and law enforcement agencies. LulzSec was responsible for various attacks, including the breach of Sony Pictures Entertainment, the hacking of the CIA website, and the leak of classified documents from Stratfor.

4. Legal and Ethical Considerations:

Hacktivism raises various legal and ethical considerations related to freedom of expression, privacy, cybersecurity, and the rule of law. While hacktivists may justify their actions as a form of civil disobedience, protest, or resistance against perceived injustices, their activities may also violate laws related to unauthorized access, computer fraud, intellectual property infringement, or cyber terrorism, depending on the nature and impact of their actions.

5. Countermeasures and Mitigation:

Defending against hacktivism requires a combination of technical controls, legal measures, and social interventions to prevent, detect, and mitigate the risks posed by hacktivist attacks. Some countermeasures and mitigation strategies include:

a) **Cybersecurity Measures:** Organizations should implement robust cybersecurity controls, such as firewalls, intrusion detection systems (IDS), intrusion prevention systems (IPS), web application firewalls (WAF), and endpoint security solutions, to protect against hacktivist attacks, data breaches, or website defacements.

b) **Incident Response Plans:** Organizations should develop incident response plans, playbooks, and procedures to quickly detect, contain, and respond to hacktivist attacks, minimize damage, and restore normal operations in the event of a security breach or data breach.

c) **Legal Remedies:** Law enforcement agencies should investigate hacktivist attacks, identify perpetrators, and prosecute individuals or groups responsible for illegal activities, such as unauthorized access, data theft, or cyber vandalism, to enforce the rule of law and deter future attacks.

d) **Dialogue and Engagement:** Governments, corporations, and institutions should engage with hacktivist groups, activists, or whistle blowers through dialogue, negotiation, or mediation to address grievances, resolve conflicts, or address underlying issues driving hacktivist actions.

Hacktivism represents a complex and evolving phenomenon that blurs the lines between activism, protest, and cybercrime, as hacktivists leverage hacking skills to advance political, social, or ideological causes through cyber attacks, data breaches, or online activism. While hacktivism raises important issues related to freedom of expression, civil liberties, and social justice, it also poses risks to cybersecurity, privacy, and the rule of law, as hacktivist attacks can disrupt operations, compromise sensitive information, or cause reputational damage to targeted organizations or individuals. By understanding the motivations, tactics, and implications of hacktivism, organizations and governments can better prepare for and respond to the challenges posed by hacktivist groups in the digital age.

Cyber criminals

Cyber criminals represent a diverse and dynamic category of malicious actors who engage in a wide range of criminal activities in the digital domain, including hacking, malware distribution, identity theft, fraud, extortion, and online scams. Motivated by financial gain, personal profit, or malicious intent, cyber criminals exploit vulnerabilities in computer systems, networks, and software to steal sensitive information, compromise user accounts, or disrupt online services for illicit purposes. In this section, we'll explore in detail the nature of cyber criminals, their motivations, tactics, techniques, and the implications for cybersecurity, privacy, and digital trust in the modern era.

1. **Motivations and Objectives:**

Cyber criminals are motivated by various factors, including:

- a) **Financial Gain:** Many cyber criminals are driven by the prospect of financial gain and seek to profit from their illicit activities through activities such as ransomware attacks, credit card fraud, online banking scams, or cryptocurrency theft.

b) **Personal Profit:** Some cyber criminals engage in cybercrime for personal profit or enrichment, seeking to exploit vulnerabilities in online platforms, digital marketplaces, or e-commerce websites to sell stolen goods, counterfeit products, or illegal services.

c) **Malicious Intent:** Some cyber criminals engage in cybercrime for malicious intent or revenge, seeking to cause harm, disrupt operations, or damage the reputation of targeted individuals, organizations, or institutions through activities such as hacking, doxing, or cyber vandalism.

d) **Espionage or Sabotage:** Some cyber criminals may be motivated by espionage or sabotage objectives, seeking to steal sensitive information, intellectual property, or trade secrets from rival companies, government agencies, or foreign adversaries for strategic or competitive advantage.

2. **Tactics and Techniques:**

Cyber criminals employ a variety of tactics and techniques to achieve their objectives, including:

a) **Malware Distribution:** Cyber criminals use malware, such as viruses, worms, Trojans, ransomware, or spyware, to compromise computer systems, steal data, or extort money from victims by encrypting their files or locking their devices.

b) **Phishing and Social Engineering:** Cyber criminals use phishing emails, fake websites, or social engineering techniques to trick individuals into revealing sensitive information, such as login credentials, credit card numbers, or personal data, for identity theft or fraud.

c) **Exploiting Software Vulnerabilities:** Cyber criminals exploit vulnerabilities in software, operating systems, or web applications to gain unauthorized access to systems, execute malicious code, or steal sensitive information through techniques such as SQL injection, buffer overflow, or remote code execution.

d) **Distributed Denial-of-Service (DDoS) Attacks:** Cyber criminals launch DDoS attacks against websites, servers, or online services to disrupt operations, render them inaccessible to users, or extort money from victims by threatening to overwhelm their infrastructure with large volumes of traffic or requests.

e) **Cryptojacking:** Cyber criminals use cryptojacking malware to hijack the computing resources of infected devices, such as computers, smartphones, or IoT devices, to mine cryptocurrency without the knowledge or consent of their owners, generating profits for the attackers.

3. **Cyber Criminal Groups and Organizations:**

Cyber criminals may operate individually or as part of organized criminal groups, cybercrime syndicates, or underground marketplaces that specialize in various types of cybercrime, including:

a) **Cybercrime Syndicates:** Organized groups of cyber criminals, often operating across multiple jurisdictions, who collaborate to conduct cyber attacks, distribute malware, launder money, or engage in other illicit activities for financial gain.

- b) **Botnet Operators:** Cyber criminals who control networks of compromised computers, known as botnets, to launch DDoS attacks, distribute spam emails, or steal sensitive information from victims through techniques such as keylogging or credential harvesting.

- c) **Carding Forums:** Online forums or marketplaces where cyber criminals buy and sell stolen credit card data, payment card information, or personal identities for fraudulent purposes, such as making unauthorized purchases or committing identity theft.

- d) **Ransomware-as-a-Service (RaaS) Providers:** Criminal organizations that offer ransomware-as-a-service platforms to other cyber criminals, allowing them to distribute ransomware to victims and share profits with the service provider in exchange for access to the ransomware infrastructure and support services.

4. Legal and Regulatory Challenges:

Cyber crime poses significant legal and regulatory challenges for law enforcement agencies, governments, and international organizations, including:

- a) **Jurisdictional Issues:** Cyber crime often transcends national borders, making it difficult for law enforcement agencies to investigate, prosecute, or extradite cyber criminals who operate in jurisdictions with different laws, regulations, or enforcement capabilities.

- b) **Legal Frameworks:** Legal frameworks related to cyber crime vary widely across countries and regions, leading to inconsistencies in definitions, penalties, and enforcement mechanisms for cyber crimes, hindering international cooperation and coordination efforts.

c) **Digital Forensics:** Investigating cyber crimes requires specialized skills, tools, and techniques for digital forensics, evidence collection, and attribution, as cyber criminals may use encryption, anonymization, or obfuscation techniques to conceal their identities and cover their tracks.

d) **International Cooperation:** Combatting cyber crime requires international cooperation and collaboration among law enforcement agencies, governments, and private sector stakeholders to share threat intelligence, exchange best practices, and coordinate response efforts across borders.

5. Countermeasures and Mitigation:

Defending against cyber crime requires a multi-faceted approach that includes:

a) **Cybersecurity Awareness:** Educating individuals, organizations, and employees about common cyber threats, phishing scams, malware attacks, and best practices for cybersecurity hygiene to reduce the risk of falling victim to cyber crime.

b) **Technical Controls:** Implementing robust cybersecurity controls, such as firewalls, antivirus software, intrusion detection systems (IDS), intrusion prevention systems (IPS), and endpoint security solutions, to detect, prevent, and mitigate the impact of cyber attacks.

c) **Incident Response:** Developing incident response plans, playbooks, and procedures to quickly detect, contain, and respond to cyber security incidents, minimize damage, and restore normal operations in the event of a cyber attack or data breach.

d) Law Enforcement Cooperation: Strengthening cooperation and coordination among law enforcement agencies, governments, and international organizations to investigate cyber crimes, disrupt cyber criminal networks, and prosecute perpetrators to deter future attacks.

Cyber criminals pose a significant and evolving threat to cybersecurity, privacy, and digital trust in the modern era, as they exploit vulnerabilities in computer systems, networks, and software to steal sensitive information, compromise user accounts, or disrupt online services for financial gain, personal profit, or malicious intent. Defending against cyber crime requires a comprehensive approach that includes cybersecurity awareness, technical controls, incident response capabilities, and international cooperation to mitigate the risks posed by cyber criminals and protect individuals, organizations, and societies from the adverse impacts of cyber crime in the digital age.

Chapter 6
Tricks Cyber Spies Use to Trick People

In the digital age, cyber spies employ a variety of deceptive tactics to manipulate and exploit human vulnerabilities for their nefarious purposes. From social engineering techniques to psychological manipulation, cyber spies use cunning strategies to trick individuals into disclosing sensitive information, clicking on malicious links, or downloading malware. In this chapter, we explore the tricks and techniques cyber spies use to deceive people, compromise their security, and achieve their objectives. By understanding these tactics and being aware of common scams and ploys, individuals can better protect themselves against cyber threats and safeguard their personal information and digital assets in an increasingly hostile online environment. This chapter sheds light on the deceptive methods employed by cyber spies and provides practical guidance on how to recognize and avoid falling victim to their schemes.

Phishing Attacks

Phishing attacks represent one of the most prevalent and insidious forms of cybercrime, where cyber criminals use deceptive tactics to trick individuals into revealing sensitive information, such as login credentials, financial data, or personal information, for fraudulent purposes. Phishing attacks typically involve sending fraudulent emails, text messages, or instant messages that appear to be from legitimate sources, such as banks, social media platforms, or government agencies, in an attempt to lure recipients into clicking on malicious links, downloading malware, or providing confidential information. In this section, we'll explore in detail the nature of phishing attacks, their tactics, techniques, and the implications for cybersecurity, privacy, and digital trust in the modern era.

1. Understanding Phishing Attacks:

Phishing attacks are designed to exploit human vulnerabilities and manipulate psychological triggers to deceive individuals into taking actions that benefit cyber criminals. Phishing attacks often involve the following elements:

a) **Spoofed Identities:** Phishing emails often mimic the appearance and branding of legitimate organizations or trusted sources to deceive recipients into believing that the communication is genuine.

b) **Urgent Requests:** Phishing emails often create a sense of urgency or fear by claiming that immediate action is required to resolve an issue, such as a security breach, account suspension, or fraudulent activity.

c) **Social Engineering Tactics:** Phishing attacks rely on social engineering tactics to manipulate recipients' emotions, curiosity, or trust to convince them to click on malicious links, open malicious attachments, or disclose sensitive information.

d) **Malicious Payloads:** Phishing emails may contain malicious links or attachments that, when clicked or opened, download malware onto the victim's device, such as ransomware, spyware, or keyloggers, to steal sensitive information or compromise system security.

2. Types of Phishing Attacks:

Phishing attacks come in various forms, each with its own tactics and objectives, including:

a) **Email Phishing:** Email phishing is the most common form of phishing attack, where cyber criminals send fraudulent emails posing as legitimate organizations or individuals to trick recipients into clicking on malicious links, downloading malware, or providing sensitive information.

b) **Spear Phishing:** Spear phishing attacks target specific individuals or organizations with highly personalized and convincing messages tailored to their interests, roles, or relationships to increase the likelihood of success.

c) **Whaling:** Whaling attacks target high-profile individuals, such as corporate executives, government officials, or celebrities, with fraudulent emails that impersonate senior executives or trusted contacts to deceive recipients into disclosing sensitive information or authorizing fraudulent transactions.

d) **Vishing:** Vishing attacks, or voice phishing, involve cyber criminals using phone calls or voicemail messages to impersonate legitimate entities, such as banks, government agencies, or tech support, to trick victims into providing personal information or financial details over the phone.

e) **Smishing:** Smishing attacks, or SMS phishing, involve cyber criminals sending fraudulent text messages to mobile phone users, typically containing links to malicious websites or instructions to call a phone number to verify account information or claim a prize.

3. **Implications of Phishing Attacks:**

Phishing attacks have significant implications for cybersecurity, privacy, and digital trust, including:

a) **Data Breaches:** Phishing attacks can result in data breaches, where cyber criminals steal sensitive information, such as login credentials, credit card numbers, or personal data, from unsuspecting victims, leading to identity theft, financial fraud, or reputational damage.

b) **Financial Losses:** Phishing attacks can lead to financial losses for individuals and organizations through unauthorized transactions, fraudulent wire transfers, or ransom payments to cyber criminals who extort money by encrypting files or locking devices.

c) **Compromised Systems:** Phishing attacks can compromise the security of individuals' and organizations' computer systems, networks, and devices by downloading malware onto their devices, allowing cyber criminals to access sensitive information, spy on users, or control their systems remotely.

d) **Reputation Damage:** Phishing attacks can damage the reputation and credibility of organizations targeted by cyber criminals, leading to loss of customer trust, negative publicity, or legal repercussions for failing to protect sensitive information or prevent data breaches.

4. **Countermeasures and Mitigation:**

Defending against phishing attacks requires a multi-faceted approach that includes:

a) **Security Awareness Training:** Educating individuals and employees about common phishing tactics, warning signs, and best practices for identifying and avoiding phishing attacks, such as scrutinizing email addresses, verifying sender identities, and avoiding clicking on suspicious links or attachments.

- b) **Email Filtering and Authentication:** Deploying email filtering solutions and authentication mechanisms, such as Domain-based Message Authentication, Reporting, and Conformance (DMARC), Sender Policy Framework (SPF), and Domain Keys Identified Mail (DKIM), to detect and block phishing emails before they reach recipients' inboxes.

- c) **Endpoint Security Solutions:** Implementing endpoint security solutions, such as antivirus software, firewalls, intrusion detection systems (IDS), intrusion prevention systems (IPS), and email security gateways, to detect and block malicious attachments, links, or payloads delivered through phishing emails.

- d) **Two-Factor Authentication (2FA):** Enabling two-factor authentication (2FA) or multi-factor authentication (MFA) on online accounts and services to add an extra layer of security and verification beyond passwords, reducing the risk of unauthorized access in the event of compromised credentials.

5. Continuous Monitoring and Response:

Organizations should continuously monitor their networks, systems, and endpoints for signs of phishing attacks, unusual activity, or unauthorized access and respond promptly to suspected incidents by:

- a) **Incident Detection:** Implementing security monitoring tools, threat intelligence feeds, and intrusion detection systems (IDS) to detect phishing attacks, suspicious behavior, or indicators of compromise (IOCs) on their networks and systems.

- b) **Incident Response:** Developing incident response plans, playbooks, and procedures to quickly detect, contain, and respond to phishing attacks, minimize damage, and restore normal operations in the event of a security breach or data breach.

c) **Post-Incident Analysis:** Conducting post-incident analysis, forensic investigations, or root cause analysis to identify the source, scope, and impact of phishing attacks, gather evidence, and implement corrective actions to prevent future incidents.

Phishing attacks pose a significant and pervasive threat to cybersecurity, privacy, and digital trust in the modern era, as cyber criminals continue to exploit human vulnerabilities and manipulate psychological triggers to deceive individuals and organizations for fraudulent purposes. Defending against phishing attacks requires a proactive and multi-layered approach that includes security awareness training, email filtering, endpoint security solutions, two-factor authentication, continuous monitoring, and incident response capabilities to detect, prevent, and mitigate the risks posed by phishing attacks and protect individuals, organizations, and societies from the adverse impacts of cybercrime in the digital age.

Social Engineering

Social engineering is a technique used by cyber criminals to manipulate individuals into divulging confidential information, performing actions, or providing access to sensitive systems or data through psychological manipulation, deception, and manipulation of human behavior. Unlike traditional hacking methods that rely on exploiting technical vulnerabilities, social engineering exploits the weakest link in the security chain: human psychology. In this section, we'll delve into the intricacies of social engineering, its tactics, techniques, and the implications for cybersecurity, privacy, and digital trust in the modern era.

1. **Understanding Social Engineering:**

Social engineering is a form of manipulation that preys on human emotions, trust, and cognitive biases to trick individuals into disclosing sensitive information or performing actions that benefit cyber criminals. Social engineers often exploit various psychological principles, such as authority, urgency, scarcity, and reciprocity, to manipulate their targets and bypass security defenses. Social engineering attacks can take many forms, including:

   a) **Phishing:** Social engineers use fraudulent emails, text messages, or instant messages to impersonate trusted entities, such as banks, government agencies, or coworkers, and trick recipients into clicking on malicious links, downloading malware, or revealing sensitive information.

   b) **Pretexting:** Social engineers create elaborate pretexts or fictional scenarios to gain the trust of their targets, such as posing as tech support personnel, delivery drivers, or job applicants, to trick them into divulging personal information or granting access to restricted areas.

   c) **Baiting:** Social engineers entice their targets with tempting offers or rewards, such as free software downloads, gift cards, or concert tickets, to lure them into clicking on malicious links, opening infected files, or sharing their login credentials.

   d) **Impersonation:** Social engineers impersonate trusted individuals or authority figures, such as executives, employees, or IT administrators, to manipulate their targets into complying with their requests, such as transferring funds, changing passwords, or revealing sensitive information.

e) **Tailgating:** Social engineers exploit physical security weaknesses by following authorized individuals into restricted areas, such as office buildings or data centers, without proper authorization or identification, to gain unauthorized access to sensitive information or systems.

2. Psychological Principles:

Social engineering attacks leverage various psychological principles and cognitive biases to influence human behavior and elicit desired responses from their targets. Some common psychological principles exploited by social engineers include:

a) **Reciprocity:** Social engineers offer something of value, such as a free gift or special offer, to create a sense of obligation in their targets, increasing the likelihood that they will comply with their requests in return.

b) **Authority:** Social engineers pose as authority figures, such as supervisors, managers, or law enforcement officers, to gain the trust and compliance of their targets, who are more likely to obey orders from perceived authority figures.

c) **Scarcity:** Social engineers create a sense of urgency or scarcity by claiming that opportunities or rewards are limited or time-sensitive, encouraging their targets to act quickly without thoroughly evaluating the risks or consequences.

d) **Familiarity:** Social engineers mimic the language, tone, and style of communication used by their targets' friends, colleagues, or acquaintances to create a sense of familiarity and trust, making it easier to deceive them into complying with their requests.

e) **Consistency:** Social engineers exploit the human tendency to be consistent with past commitments or actions by gradually escalating their requests or manipulations over time, making it harder for their targets to refuse or back out.

3. Implications of Social Engineering:

Social engineering attacks have significant implications for cybersecurity, privacy, and digital trust, including:

a) **Data Breaches:** Social engineering attacks can lead to data breaches, where cyber criminals steal sensitive information, such as login credentials, financial data, or personal information, from unsuspecting victims, leading to identity theft, financial fraud, or reputational damage.

b) **Financial Losses:** Social engineering attacks can result in financial losses for individuals and organizations through unauthorized transactions, fraudulent wire transfers, or ransom payments to cyber criminals who extort money by encrypting files or locking devices.

c) **Reputation Damage:** Social engineering attacks can damage the reputation and credibility of organizations targeted by cyber criminals, leading to loss of customer trust, negative publicity, or legal repercussions for failing to protect sensitive information or prevent data breaches.

d) **Trust Erosion:** Social engineering attacks erode trust and confidence in digital communications, online interactions, and electronic transactions, as individuals become more wary of fraudulent emails, phishing scams, or deceptive tactics used by cyber criminals to exploit their vulnerabilities.

4. Countermeasures and Mitigation:

Defending against social engineering attacks requires a multi-faceted approach that includes:

a) **Security Awareness Training:** Educating individuals and employees about common social engineering tactics, warning signs, and best practices for identifying and avoiding social engineering attacks, such as verifying the identity of senders, questioning requests, and reporting suspicious behavior.

b) **Email Filtering and Authentication:** Deploying email filtering solutions and authentication mechanisms, such as Domain-based Message Authentication, Reporting, and Conformance (DMARC), Sender Policy Framework (SPF), and DomainKeys Identified Mail (DKIM), to detect and block phishing emails before they reach recipients' inboxes.

c) **Endpoint Security Solutions:** Implementing endpoint security solutions, such as antivirus software, firewalls, intrusion detection systems (IDS), intrusion prevention systems (IPS), and email security gateways, to detect and block malicious attachments, links, or payloads delivered through social engineering attacks.

d) **Two-Factor Authentication (2FA):** Enabling two-factor authentication (2FA) or multi-factor authentication (MFA) on online accounts and services to add an extra layer of security and verification beyond passwords, reducing the risk of unauthorized access in the event of compromised credentials.

5. **Continuous Monitoring and Response:**

Organizations should continuously monitor their networks, systems, and endpoints for signs of social engineering attacks, unusual activity, or unauthorized access and respond promptly to suspected incidents by:

a) **Incident Detection:** Implementing security monitoring tools, threat intelligence feeds, and intrusion detection systems (IDS) to detect social engineering attacks, suspicious behavior, or indicators of compromise (IOCs) on their networks and systems.

b) **Incident Response:** Developing incident response plans, playbooks, and procedures to quickly detect, contain, and respond to social engineering attacks, minimize damage, and restore normal operations in the event of a security breach or data breach.

c) **Post-Incident Analysis:** Conducting post-incident analysis, forensic investigations, or root cause analysis to identify the source, scope, and impact of social engineering attacks, gather evidence, and implement corrective actions to prevent future incidents.

Social engineering represents a significant and persistent threat to cybersecurity, privacy, and digital trust in the modern era, as cyber criminals continue to exploit human vulnerabilities and manipulate psychological triggers to deceive individuals and organizations for fraudulent purposes. Defending against social engineering attacks requires a proactive and multi-layered approach that includes security awareness training, email filtering, endpoint security solutions, two-factor authentication, continuous monitoring, and incident response capabilities to detect, prevent, and mitigate the risks posed by social engineering attacks and protect individuals, organizations, and societies from the adverse impacts of cybercrime in the digital age.

Spoofing and Impersonation

Spoofing and impersonation are two common tactics used by cyber criminals to deceive individuals and organizations for malicious purposes. While they may sound similar, they involve distinct methods and objectives. In this section, we'll delve into the intricacies of spoofing and impersonation, their tactics, techniques, and the implications for cybersecurity, privacy, and digital trust in the modern era.

1. Understanding Spoofing:

Spoofing is a technique used by cyber criminals to impersonate or masquerade as another entity, such as a person, organization, or device, by falsifying information or manipulating digital communications. Spoofing attacks typically involve the following elements:

a) **Email Spoofing:** Email spoofing involves forging the sender's email address in an email header to make it appear as if the message originated from a trusted source, such as a legitimate organization or individual. Cyber criminals use email spoofing to deceive recipients into opening malicious attachments, clicking on phishing links, or disclosing sensitive information.

b) **IP Address Spoofing:** IP address spoofing involves falsifying the source IP address in network packets to conceal the identity or location of the sender and evade detection by network security measures, such as firewalls or intrusion detection systems (IDS). Cyber criminals use IP address spoofing to launch distributed denial-of-service (DDoS) attacks, bypass access controls, or mask their malicious activities.

c) **Caller ID Spoofing:** Caller ID spoofing involves falsifying the caller ID information displayed on a recipient's phone to disguise the caller's identity or impersonate a trusted entity, such as a bank, government agency, or tech support provider. Cyber criminals use caller ID spoofing to conduct vishing (voice phishing) scams, impersonate legitimate businesses, or deceive victims into providing personal information or financial details over the phone.

d) **Website Spoofing:** Website spoofing involves creating fake or fraudulent websites that mimic the appearance and functionality of legitimate websites to trick users into entering sensitive information, such as login credentials, credit card numbers, or personal data. Cyber criminals use website spoofing to conduct phishing attacks, steal user credentials, or distribute malware to unsuspecting victims.

2. Understanding Impersonation:

Impersonation is a tactic used by cyber criminals to impersonate or mimic trusted individuals, such as executives, employees, or customers, to deceive recipients into complying with their requests or divulging sensitive information. Impersonation attacks typically involve the following elements:

a) **CEO Fraud:** CEO fraud, also known as business email compromise (BEC) or executive impersonation, involves cyber criminals impersonating company executives, such as CEOs or CFOs, to trick employees into initiating wire transfers, making fraudulent payments, or disclosing sensitive information. CEO fraud attacks often target finance departments, accounts payable staff, or individuals with access to financial systems.

b) **Employee Impersonation:** Employee impersonation involves cyber criminals impersonating employees or coworkers within an organization to gain unauthorized access to sensitive information, compromise internal systems, or conduct fraudulent activities. Employee impersonation attacks may involve creating fake email accounts, social media profiles, or instant messaging accounts to deceive colleagues or collaborators.

c) **Customer Impersonation:** Customer impersonation involves cyber criminals impersonating customers, clients, or service users to deceive employees or customer service representatives into providing sensitive information, resetting account passwords, or authorizing unauthorized transactions. Customer impersonation attacks may target call centers, help desks, or support channels to exploit vulnerabilities in customer authentication processes.

3. **Implications of Spoofing and Impersonation:**

Spoofing and impersonation attacks have significant implications for cybersecurity, privacy, and digital trust, including:

a) **Data Breaches:** Spoofing and impersonation attacks can lead to data breaches, where cyber criminals steal sensitive information, such as login credentials, financial data, or personal information, from unsuspecting victims, leading to identity theft, financial fraud, or reputational damage.

b) **Financial Losses:** Spoofing and impersonation attacks can result in financial losses for individuals and organizations through unauthorized transactions, fraudulent wire transfers, or ransom payments to cyber criminals who exploit vulnerabilities in authentication processes or social engineering tactics.

c) **Reputation Damage:** Spoofing and impersonation attacks can damage the reputation and credibility of organizations targeted by cyber criminals, leading to loss of customer trust, negative publicity, or legal repercussions for failing to protect sensitive information or prevent data breaches.

d) **Trust Erosion:** Spoofing and impersonation attacks erode trust and confidence in digital communications, online interactions, and electronic transactions, as individuals become more wary of fraudulent emails, phishing scams, or deceptive tactics used by cyber criminals to exploit their vulnerabilities.

4. **Countermeasures and Mitigation:**

Defending against spoofing and impersonation attacks requires a multi-faceted approach that includes:

a) **Security Awareness Training:** Educating individuals and employees about common spoofing and impersonation tactics, warning signs, and best practices for identifying and avoiding social engineering attacks, such as verifying sender identities, questioning requests, and reporting suspicious behavior.

b) **Email Filtering and Authentication:** Deploying email filtering solutions and authentication mechanisms, such as Domain-based Message Authentication, Reporting, and Conformance (DMARC), Sender Policy Framework (SPF), and DomainKeys Identified Mail (DKIM), to detect and block spoofed emails before they reach recipients' inboxes.

c) **Caller ID Verification:** Implementing caller ID verification solutions or call authentication mechanisms to verify the authenticity of incoming calls and detect caller ID spoofing attempts before answering or engaging with unknown callers.

d) **Two-Factor Authentication (2FA):** Enabling two-factor authentication (2FA) or multi-factor authentication (MFA) on online accounts and services to add an extra layer of security and verification beyond passwords, reducing the risk of unauthorized access in the event of compromised credentials.

5. Continuous Monitoring and Response:

Organizations should continuously monitor their networks, systems, and endpoints for signs of spoofing and impersonation attacks, unusual activity, or unauthorized access and respond promptly to suspected incidents by:

   a) **Incident Detection:** Implementing security monitoring tools, threat intelligence feeds, and intrusion detection systems (IDS) to detect spoofing and impersonation attacks, suspicious behavior, or indicators of compromise (IOCs) on their networks and systems.

   b) **b. Incident Response:** Developing incident response plans, playbooks, and procedures to quickly detect, contain, and respond to spoofing and impersonation attacks, minimize damage, and restore normal operations in the event of a security breach or data breach.

   c) **Post-Incident Analysis:** Conducting post-incident analysis, forensic investigations, or root cause analysis to identify the source, scope, and impact of spoofing and impersonation attacks, gather evidence, and implement corrective actions to prevent future incidents.

Spoofing and impersonation represent significant and persistent threats to cybersecurity, privacy, and digital trust in the modern era, as cyber criminals continue to exploit vulnerabilities in authentication processes, social engineering tactics, and human behavior to deceive individuals and organizations for malicious purposes. Defending against spoofing and impersonation attacks requires a proactive and multi-layered approach that includes security awareness training, email filtering, authentication mechanisms, two-factor authentication, continuous monitoring, and incident response capabilities to detect, prevent, and mitigate the risks posed by spoofing and impersonation attacks and protect individuals, organizations, and societies from the adverse impacts of cybercrime in the digital age.

Chapter 7
Who Cyber Spies Target

In the digital landscape, cyber spies cast a wide net, targeting individuals, organizations, and governments across various sectors and industries. Understanding the profiles of their targets provides insight into the motives, methods, and impact of cyber espionage activities. In this chapter, we delve into the diverse range of entities targeted by cyber spies, ranging from high-profile government agencies to unsuspecting individuals, and explore the reasons behind these targeting decisions. By shedding light on the demographics, vulnerabilities, and motivations of cyber espionage targets, we aim to enhance awareness and resilience against these pervasive threats in the digital age. This chapter illuminates the dynamics of cyber espionage targeting, highlighting the critical role of cybersecurity vigilance and preparedness in safeguarding against the ever-evolving tactics of cyber spies.

Government Agencies

Government agencies are among the prime targets for cyber spies due to their significant roles in national security, governance, and policymaking. These entities possess vast amounts of sensitive information, including classified data, intelligence reports, diplomatic communications, and citizen records, making them lucrative targets for cyber espionage activities. In this section, we'll delve into the specific challenges faced by government agencies in defending against cyber espionage, the tactics used by cyber spies to target them, and the implications for national security and public trust.

1. **The Significance of Government Agencies:**

Government agencies play critical roles in upholding national security, law enforcement, public safety, and regulatory compliance. These entities are responsible for safeguarding sensitive information, protecting critical infrastructure, and ensuring the smooth functioning of essential services. Government agencies handle a wide range of data, including classified information, intelligence reports, diplomatic communications, and citizen records, making them attractive targets for cyber spies seeking to obtain valuable intelligence, disrupt operations, or undermine national interests.

2. **Challenges Faced by Government Agencies:**

Government agencies face numerous challenges in defending against cyber espionage, including:

a) **Complexity of Networks:** Government agencies operate complex IT infrastructures comprising interconnected networks, systems, and applications, which present multiple entry points and vulnerabilities for cyber attackers to exploit.

b) **Resource Constraints:** Government agencies often face resource constraints, including limited budgets, understaffed IT departments, and outdated technologies, making it challenging to implement robust cybersecurity measures and maintain effective defense capabilities.

c) **High-Value Targets:** Government agencies possess valuable assets, including classified information, intellectual property, and sensitive data, which make them attractive targets for cyber espionage activities by nation-states, foreign adversaries, or criminal organizations seeking to gain a strategic advantage or further their geopolitical objectives.

d) **Sophisticated Threat Actors:** Government agencies are targeted by sophisticated threat actors, including nation-state-sponsored hackers, cybercriminal groups, and hacktivist organizations, who employ advanced tactics, techniques, and procedures (TTPs) to evade detection, bypass security controls, and infiltrate targeted networks undetected.

e) **Regulatory Compliance:** Government agencies must comply with stringent regulatory requirements, privacy laws, and cybersecurity standards, such as the Federal Information Security Management Act (FISMA) in the United States, which mandate the implementation of comprehensive cybersecurity measures, risk assessments, and incident response protocols to protect sensitive information and mitigate cyber risks.

3. **Tactics Used by Cyber Spies:**

Cyber spies employ various tactics to target government agencies, including:

a) **Phishing and Social Engineering:** Cyber spies use phishing emails, spear phishing campaigns, and social engineering tactics to deceive government employees into clicking on malicious links, opening infected attachments, or disclosing sensitive information, such as login credentials or access codes.

b) **Malware and Ransomware:** Cyber spies deploy malware, ransomware, and other malicious software to compromise government networks, steal sensitive data, or disrupt critical services. These malware variants may include remote access trojans (RATs), key loggers, and data exfiltration tools designed to covertly collect and exfiltrate classified information.

c) **Supply Chain Attacks:** Cyber spies target government agencies through supply chain attacks, where they compromise third-party vendors, contractors, or service providers to gain unauthorized access to government networks, systems, or data repositories. Supply chain attacks pose significant risks to government agencies, as they often involve trusted partners or suppliers with privileged access to sensitive information.

d) **Zero-Day Exploits:** Cyber spies exploit zero-day vulnerabilities in software applications, operating systems, or network protocols to launch targeted attacks against government agencies. Zero-day exploits enable cyber attackers to bypass security controls, evade detection, and gain unauthorized access to government networks, systems, or databases before vendors can release patches or updates to remediate the vulnerabilities.

e) **Insider Threats:** Cyber spies recruit insiders, such as disgruntled employees, contractors, or trusted personnel with access to sensitive information, to steal classified data, leak confidential documents, or sabotage government operations from within. Insider threats pose significant challenges to government agencies, as they often involve trusted insiders with legitimate access privileges, making them harder to detect and mitigate.

4. Implications for National Security:

Cyber espionage targeting government agencies has profound implications for national security, including:

a) **Loss of Sensitive Information:** Cyber espionage attacks targeting government agencies can result in the loss or compromise of sensitive information, including classified data, intelligence reports, diplomatic communications, and national security secrets, which may undermine national interests, compromise diplomatic relations, or jeopardize strategic alliances.

b) **Disruption of Operations:** Cyber espionage attacks can disrupt government operations, critical infrastructure, and essential services, causing disruptions to public safety, law enforcement, emergency response, and regulatory enforcement efforts. Disruptions to government services can have far-reaching consequences, affecting citizens, businesses, and government agencies' ability to fulfill their mandates effectively.

c) **Erosion of Public Trust:** Cyber espionage attacks targeting government agencies erode public trust and confidence in government institutions, as citizens become increasingly concerned about the security, integrity, and privacy of their personal information, government services, and democratic processes. Breaches of government data can erode public trust in government agencies' ability to protect sensitive information and uphold transparency, accountability, and trustworthiness.

d) **Geopolitical Ramifications:** Cyber espionage targeting government agencies can have geopolitical ramifications, as nation-states engage in cyber warfare, intelligence gathering, and strategic maneuvering to advance their geopolitical objectives, assert influence on the global stage, or undermine the security and stability of rival nations.

5. **Mitigation Strategies:**

To mitigate the risks posed by cyber espionage targeting government agencies, organizations can implement the following strategies:

a) **Cybersecurity Awareness Training:** Educate government employees about the risks of cyber espionage, phishing attacks, social engineering tactics, and other common threats, and provide training on how to recognize, report, and mitigate cyber threats effectively.

b) **Robust Cybersecurity Controls:** Implement robust cybersecurity controls, including network segmentation, access controls, intrusion detection systems (IDS), intrusion prevention systems (IPS), endpoint security solutions, and data encryption, to protect government networks, systems, and data from cyber espionage attacks.

c) **Continuous Monitoring and Threat Intelligence:** Implement continuous monitoring solutions and threat intelligence feeds to detect, analyze, and respond to cyber espionage activities targeting government agencies in real-time. Proactively identify indicators of compromise (IOCs), anomalous behavior, and suspicious activities to prevent data breaches or unauthorized access.

d) **Collaboration and Information Sharing:** Foster collaboration and information sharing among government agencies, law enforcement agencies, intelligence agencies, and private sector partners to exchange threat intelligence, best practices, and cyber defense strategies for combating cyber espionage effectively.

Government agencies are prime targets for cyber espionage due to their significant roles in national security, governance, and policymaking. Cyber spies employ sophisticated tactics, such as phishing, malware, supply chain attacks, and insider threats, to target government agencies and steal sensitive information, disrupt operations, or undermine national interests. Defending against cyber espionage requires a multi-faceted approach that includes robust cybersecurity controls, continuous monitoring, threat intelligence, collaboration, and information sharing to detect, prevent, and mitigate the risks posed by cyber espionage attacks and protect national security, public trust, and democratic values in the digital age.

Corporations

Corporations represent lucrative targets for cyber spies due to their vast wealth of intellectual property, proprietary information, financial data, and customer records. These entities operate in highly competitive environments, where maintaining a competitive edge and protecting sensitive information are paramount. In this section, we'll explore the specific challenges faced by corporations in defending against cyber espionage, the tactics used by cyber spies to target them, and the implications for business continuity, reputation, and customer trust.

1. The Significance of Corporations:

Corporations play a vital role in the global economy, driving innovation, economic growth, and job creation. These entities range from small startups to multinational conglomerates, operating across various sectors and industries, including technology, finance, healthcare, manufacturing, and retail. Corporations possess valuable assets, including intellectual property, trade secrets, customer data, financial records, and proprietary technologies, making them attractive targets for cyber espionage activities by nation-state actors, foreign adversaries, cybercriminal groups, and corporate competitors seeking to gain a competitive advantage, steal valuable information, or disrupt business operations.

2. Challenges Faced by Corporations:

Corporations face numerous challenges in defending against cyber espionage, including:

a) **Complexity of IT Environments:** Corporations operate complex IT infrastructures comprising interconnected networks, systems, and applications, spanning multiple locations, subsidiaries, and business units, which present numerous entry points and vulnerabilities for cyber attackers to exploit.

b) **Protection of Intellectual Property:** Corporations invest significant resources in research and development (R&D) to develop proprietary technologies, products, and services that provide them with a competitive edge in the marketplace. Protecting intellectual property (IP) from theft, infringement, or unauthorized disclosure is a top priority for corporations, as it represents a significant source of value and differentiation.

c) **Cybersecurity Budget Constraints:** Corporations often face budget constraints and resource limitations when it comes to cybersecurity, as they must balance the costs of implementing robust security measures against the potential risks of cyber threats and data breaches. Limited cybersecurity budgets may lead to gaps in security defenses, inadequate threat detection capabilities, or delays in implementing security updates and patches.

d) **Supply Chain Risks:** Corporations rely on a vast network of suppliers, vendors, contractors, and partners to deliver goods and services, which introduces supply chain risks and dependencies that can be exploited by cyber spies. Supply chain attacks targeting third-party vendors or service providers can result in data breaches, supply chain disruptions, or unauthorized access to corporate networks and systems.

e) **Regulatory Compliance Obligations:** Corporations must comply with a myriad of regulatory requirements, industry standards, and data protection laws governing the collection, storage, processing, and transmission of sensitive information, such as the General Data Protection Regulation (GDPR), Payment Card Industry Data Security Standard (PCI DSS), and Health Insurance Portability and Accountability Act (HIPAA). Failure to comply with regulatory requirements can result in hefty fines, legal liabilities, and reputational damage for corporations.

3. **Tactics Used by Cyber Spies:**

Cyber spies employ various tactics to target corporations, including:

a) **Phishing and Business Email Compromise (BEC):** Cyber spies use phishing emails, spear phishing campaigns, and BEC scams to trick employees into clicking on malicious links, opening infected attachments, or disclosing sensitive information, such as login credentials, financial data, or corporate secrets. Phishing attacks targeting corporations often impersonate trusted entities, such as executives, colleagues, or business partners, to deceive recipients and bypass security defenses.

b) **Malware and Ransomware:** Cyber spies deploy malware, ransomware, and other malicious software to infiltrate corporate networks, steal sensitive information, or disrupt business operations. Malware variants, such as ransomware, spyware, trojans, and remote access tools (RATs), may be used to encrypt files, exfiltrate data, or establish persistent access to corporate systems for espionage purposes.

c) **Insider Threats:** Cyber spies recruit insiders, such as disgruntled employees, contractors, or trusted personnel with access to sensitive information, to steal proprietary data, leak confidential documents, or sabotage corporate operations from within. Insider threats pose significant challenges to corporations, as they often involve trusted insiders with legitimate access privileges, making them harder to detect and mitigate.

d) **Supply Chain Attacks:** Cyber spies target corporations through supply chain attacks, where they compromise third-party vendors, contractors, or service providers to gain unauthorized access to corporate networks, systems, or data repositories. Supply chain attacks pose significant risks to corporations, as they often involve trusted partners or suppliers with privileged access to sensitive information.

4. **Implications for Business Continuity and Reputation:**

Cyber espionage targeting corporations has profound implications for business continuity, reputation, and customer trust, including:

a) **Disruption of Operations:** Cyber espionage attacks can disrupt corporate operations, critical business processes, and essential services, causing disruptions to production, supply chains, and customer service delivery. Disruptions to business operations can result in financial losses, reputational damage, and loss of market share for corporations, as customers, partners, and investors lose confidence in their ability to fulfill obligations and meet expectations.

b) **Loss of Intellectual Property:** Cyber espionage attacks can result in the theft, loss, or compromise of valuable intellectual property, trade secrets, and proprietary information, undermining corporations' competitive advantage, market position, and innovation capabilities. Loss of intellectual property can result in revenue losses, market share erosion, and diminished brand value for corporations, as competitors gain access to confidential information and leverage it to their advantage.

c) **Reputational Damage:** Cyber espionage attacks targeting corporations can damage their reputation, credibility, and trustworthiness in the eyes of customers, partners, regulators, and stakeholders. Breaches of customer data, data breaches, or cybersecurity incidents can erode public trust in corporations' ability to protect sensitive information, uphold privacy rights, and maintain cybersecurity standards, leading to negative publicity, legal liabilities, and customer defections.

d) **Legal and Regulatory Consequences:** Cyber espionage attacks targeting corporations can have legal and regulatory consequences, as corporations may face lawsuits, regulatory investigations, fines, or penalties for failing to protect sensitive information, comply with data protection laws, or mitigate cyber risks effectively. Failure to address cybersecurity vulnerabilities, data breaches, or compliance deficiencies can result in legal liabilities, reputational damage, and financial penalties for corporations.

5. **Mitigation Strategies:**

To mitigate the risks posed by cyber espionage targeting corporations, organizations can implement the following strategies:

a) **Comprehensive Cybersecurity Framework:** Implement a comprehensive cybersecurity framework, such as the NIST Cybersecurity Framework or ISO/IEC 27001, to establish governance, risk management, and cybersecurity controls that address the specific threats and vulnerabilities faced by corporations.

b) **Employee Training and Awareness:** Provide ongoing cybersecurity training and awareness programs to educate employees about the risks of cyber espionage, phishing attacks, social engineering tactics, and other common threats, and promote a culture of cybersecurity vigilance and accountability throughout the organization.

c) **Advanced Threat Detection:** Deploy advanced threat detection and response capabilities, such as security information and event management (SIEM) systems, endpoint detection and response (EDR) solutions, and threat intelligence platforms, to detect, analyze, and respond to cyber espionage activities targeting corporations in real-time.

d) **Third-Party Risk Management:** Implement third-party risk management programs to assess, monitor, and mitigate the cybersecurity risks posed by suppliers, vendors, contractors, and business partners, and ensure compliance with security requirements, contractual obligations, and industry standards.

Corporations are prime targets for cyber espionage due to their vast wealth of intellectual property, proprietary information, financial data, and customer records. Cyber spies employ sophisticated tactics, such as phishing, malware, insider threats, and supply chain attacks, to target corporations and steal valuable information, disrupt business operations, or undermine competitive advantages. Defending against cyber espionage requires a multi-faceted approach that includes robust cybersecurity controls, employee training, threat detection capabilities, and third-party risk management to detect, prevent, and mitigate the risks posed by cyber espionage attacks and safeguard business continuity, reputation, and customer trust in the digital age.

Individuals and Privacy

Individuals are increasingly becoming targets of cyber espionage as cybercriminals and malicious actors seek to exploit personal information for various nefarious purposes. In this section, we'll explore the specific challenges faced by individuals in defending their privacy against cyber espionage, the tactics used by cyber spies to target them, and the implications for personal security, identity theft, and digital trust.

1. **The Significance of Individuals and Privacy:**

Individuals are the most vulnerable targets for cyber espionage due to their reliance on digital technologies for communication, commerce, and social interaction. Personal privacy is a fundamental human right, enshrined in various legal frameworks and ethical principles, including the right to privacy, data protection, and digital autonomy. However, individuals face significant challenges in safeguarding their privacy against cyber espionage activities, as they often lack the technical expertise, resources, and awareness to defend against sophisticated cyber threats and privacy violations.

2. **Challenges Faced by Individuals:**

Individuals face numerous challenges in defending their privacy against cyber espionage, including:

   a) **Lack of Technical Expertise:** Many individuals lack the technical expertise or knowledge to protect themselves against cyber threats, such as phishing attacks, malware infections, and data breaches. As a result, they may inadvertently fall victim to cyber espionage activities, exposing their personal information to malicious actors.

b) **Inadequate Security Practices:** Individuals often have inadequate security practices, such as weak passwords, outdated software, and insufficient security settings, which make them easy targets for cyber spies seeking to exploit vulnerabilities in their digital defenses.

c) **Social Engineering Tactics:** Cyber spies use social engineering tactics, such as phishing emails, fake websites, and social media scams, to manipulate individuals into divulging sensitive information, such as login credentials, financial data, or personal details. Social engineering attacks prey on human psychology and emotions, exploiting trust, curiosity, and urgency to deceive unsuspecting victims.

d) **Data Privacy Concerns:** Individuals are increasingly concerned about data privacy and the protection of their personal information in the digital age, as data breaches, identity theft, and privacy violations become more prevalent. Individuals may be reluctant to share personal information online or engage in digital activities due to privacy concerns, leading to decreased trust in online platforms and services.

e) **Legal and Regulatory Protections:** Individuals rely on legal and regulatory protections, such as data protection laws, privacy regulations, and consumer rights, to safeguard their privacy rights and hold organizations accountable for privacy violations. However, enforcement mechanisms may be inadequate or ineffective in deterring cyber espionage activities or holding malicious actors accountable for privacy breaches.

3. **Tactics Used by Cyber Spies:**

Cyber spies employ various tactics to target individuals and invade their privacy, including:

a) **Phishing and Social Engineering:** Cyber spies use phishing emails, fake websites, and social media scams to trick individuals into revealing sensitive information, such as login credentials, financial data, or personal details. Phishing attacks often impersonate trusted entities, such as banks, government agencies, or online retailers, to deceive victims and steal their personal information.

b) **Malware and Spyware:** Cyber spies deploy malware, spyware, and other malicious software to infect individuals' devices, such as computers, smartphones, and tablets, and monitor their activities, steal their personal information, or hijack their devices for surveillance purposes. Malware variants, such as key loggers, remote access trojans (RATs), and spyware, may be used to collect sensitive data, record keystrokes, or capture screenshots without the victim's knowledge.

c) **Data Breaches and Identity Theft:** Cyber spies target individuals through data breaches, where they gain unauthorized access to databases, online accounts, or cloud storage services containing personal information, such as names, addresses, social security numbers, or credit card numbers. Data breaches can result in identity theft, financial fraud, or reputational damage for individuals whose personal information is exposed or compromised.

d) **Online Surveillance and Tracking:** Cyber spies conduct online surveillance and tracking of individuals' digital activities, communications, and interactions to gather intelligence, monitor their behavior, or profile their interests for targeted advertising, surveillance, or exploitation. Online surveillance techniques may involve tracking cookies, device fingerprinting, location tracking, and social media monitoring to collect data without the individual's consent or knowledge.

e) **Credential Stuffing and Account Takeovers:** Cyber spies use credential stuffing attacks to exploit reused or weak passwords and gain unauthorized access to individuals' online accounts, such as email, social media, or financial accounts. Account takeovers can lead to unauthorized transactions, data breaches, or privacy violations, as cyber spies impersonate individuals and exploit their digital identities for fraudulent purposes.

4. **Implications for Personal Security and Digital Trust:**

Cyber espionage targeting individuals has profound implications for personal security, identity protection, and digital trust, including:

a) **Identity Theft and Financial Fraud:** Cyber espionage attacks can result in identity theft, financial fraud, and unauthorized access to individuals' financial accounts, credit cards, or online profiles, leading to financial losses, credit card fraud, or reputational damage.

b) **Privacy Violations and Data Exposure:** Cyber espionage attacks can violate individuals' privacy rights and expose their personal information to unauthorized access, surveillance, or exploitation by malicious actors, leading to loss of privacy, embarrassment, or personal harm.

c) **Psychological Impact and Emotional Distress:** Cyber espionage attacks can have a psychological impact on individuals, causing emotional distress, anxiety, or paranoia about their online activities, digital privacy, and personal security. Victims of cyber espionage may experience feelings of vulnerability, distrust, or isolation as a result of privacy violations or digital intrusions.

d) **Loss of Digital Trust and Confidence:** Cyber espionage attacks erode digital trust and confidence in online platforms, services, and communication channels, as individuals become more wary of sharing personal information, engaging in online activities, or interacting with unknown entities online. Loss of digital trust can hinder digital adoption, e-commerce growth, and social connectivity, as individuals seek to protect their privacy and security in the digital age.

5. **Mitigation Strategies:**

To mitigate the risks posed by cyber espionage targeting individuals and safeguard their privacy, individuals can implement the following strategies:

a) **Cybersecurity Awareness and Education:** Stay informed about common cyber threats, phishing scams, and privacy risks, and educate yourself about best practices for protecting your personal information, securing your devices, and maintaining digital privacy and security.

b) **Strong Passwords and Security Settings:** Use strong, unique passwords for each online account, enable two-factor authentication (2FA) where available, and regularly update your security settings and privacy preferences to protect your personal information from unauthorized access or exploitation.

c) **Vigilance and Suspicion:** Be cautious of unsolicited emails, messages, or requests for personal information, and verify the legitimacy of unknown contacts, websites, or offers before sharing sensitive information or engaging in online transactions. Trust your instincts and exercise caution when interacting with unfamiliar entities online.

d) **Privacy-enhancing Tools and Technologies:** Use privacy-enhancing tools and technologies, such as virtual private networks (VPNs), ad blockers, encrypted messaging apps, and privacy-focused browsers, to protect your online privacy, anonymize your digital footprint, and prevent unauthorized tracking or surveillance.

e) **Data Protection and Privacy Practices:** Practice good data hygiene and privacy practices by minimizing the collection, retention, and sharing of personal information, regularly reviewing your privacy settings and permissions, and exercising caution when sharing sensitive information online or engaging in digital transactions.

Individuals are increasingly becoming targets of cyber espionage as cybercriminals and malicious actors seek to exploit personal information for various nefarious purposes. Defending against cyber espionage requires individuals to be vigilant, informed, and proactive about protecting their privacy, securing their devices, and maintaining digital trust in the face of evolving cyber threats and privacy risks. By implementing cybersecurity best practices, raising awareness about common cyber threats, and advocating for stronger privacy protections, individuals can mitigate the risks posed by cyber espionage and safeguard their personal security, identity, and digital autonomy in the digital age.

Chapter 8
How Cyber Spies Gather Information?

In the intricate world of cyber espionage, the gathering of information is a critical step in achieving the objectives of malicious actors. Whether it's nation-state actors seeking to gather intelligence for political or military advantage, cybercriminals aiming to steal valuable data for financial gain, or hacktivists looking to expose perceived injustices, the methods employed to gather information are diverse and ever-evolving. In this chapter, we delve into the intricate techniques and strategies used by cyber spies to gather information from their targets. From reconnaissance and social engineering to data exfiltration and open-source intelligence (OSINT) gathering, the arsenal of tools and tactics employed by cyber spies is vast and sophisticated. By understanding how cyber spies gather information, individuals, organizations, and governments can better prepare themselves to defend against cyber espionage threats and protect sensitive data and assets. This chapter aims to shed light on the clandestine world of information gathering in cyberspace and highlight the importance of vigilance, awareness, and cybersecurity measures in safeguarding against cyber espionage activities.

Data Collection Methods

Data collection methods are fundamental to cyber espionage operations, enabling cyber spies to gather valuable intelligence, steal sensitive information, and achieve their objectives. In this section, we'll explore the diverse range of methods used by cyber spies to collect data from their targets, including reconnaissance, social engineering, data exfiltration, and open-source intelligence (OSINT) gathering.

1. Reconnaissance:

Reconnaissance is the process of gathering information about a target, such as its network infrastructure, systems, vulnerabilities, and security controls, to identify potential entry points and exploit weaknesses. Cyber spies conduct reconnaissance using various techniques, including:

a) **Network Scanning:** Cyber spies use network scanning tools, such as Nmap or Nessus, to identify active hosts, open ports, and services running on target networks. Network scanning helps cyber spies map the network topology, identify potential vulnerabilities, and determine the best attack vectors for infiltration.

b) **Footprinting:** Cyber spies conduct footprinting to gather information about a target's digital footprint, including domain names, IP addresses, email addresses, and employee names. Footprinting techniques may include passive reconnaissance through public sources, such as search engines, social media profiles, and corporate websites, to collect information without alerting the target.

c) **OSINT Gathering:** Open-source intelligence (OSINT) gathering involves collecting information from publicly available sources, such as news articles, social media posts, online forums, and public databases, to gather intelligence about a target's activities, interests, and vulnerabilities. OSINT gathering provides cyber spies with valuable insights into the target's operations, personnel, and digital assets.

d) **Social Engineering:** Cyber spies use social engineering tactics, such as pretexting, phishing, and impersonation, to manipulate individuals into revealing sensitive information or granting unauthorized access to systems or data. Social engineering exploits human psychology and trust to deceive targets and extract valuable intelligence.

2. Social Engineering:

Social engineering is a psychological manipulation technique used by cyber spies to deceive individuals into divulging confidential information, such as passwords, login credentials, or financial data. Cyber spies employ various social engineering tactics, including:

a) **Phishing:** Phishing involves sending fraudulent emails, messages, or websites that appear to be from reputable sources, such as banks, government agencies, or trusted contacts, to trick individuals into disclosing sensitive information or clicking on malicious links. Phishing attacks often exploit urgency, curiosity, or fear to prompt victims to take action without verifying the authenticity of the communication.

b) **Pretexting:** Pretexting involves creating a false pretext or scenario to manipulate individuals into disclosing information or performing actions that benefit the attacker. Cyber spies may impersonate authority figures, such as IT administrators, customer service representatives, or law enforcement officers, to gain the trust of their targets and elicit sensitive information or access privileges.

c) **Baiting:** Baiting involves enticing individuals with promises of rewards or incentives, such as free software downloads, movie downloads, or gift cards, to lure them into clicking on malicious links or downloading malware-infected files. Baiting exploits human curiosity and greed to trick victims into compromising their security and privacy.

d) **Quid Pro Quo:** Quid pro quo involves offering something of value in exchange for information or assistance from the target. Cyber spies may offer technical support, software upgrades, or insider tips in exchange for login credentials, access codes, or other sensitive information from their targets.

3. Data Exfiltration:

Data exfiltration is the unauthorized transfer of data from a target's network or systems to an external location controlled by cyber spies. Data exfiltration techniques include:

a) **File Transfer:** Cyber spies use file transfer protocols, such as FTP (File Transfer Protocol) or HTTP (Hypertext Transfer Protocol), to transfer stolen data from compromised systems to external servers or cloud storage platforms. File transfer allows cyber spies to exfiltrate large volumes of data quickly and efficiently without raising suspicion.

b) **Command and Control (C&C) Channels:** Cyber spies use command and control (C&C) channels to establish covert communication channels with compromised systems and issue commands to exfiltrate data or control compromised devices remotely. C&C channels may use encrypted communication protocols, such as HTTPS or DNS (Domain Name System), to evade detection and bypass security controls.

c) **Steganography:** Steganography involves hiding sensitive data within innocent-looking files, such as images, audio files, or documents, to evade detection and bypass security controls. Cyber spies use steganography techniques to embed stolen data within digital media files and transfer them through public channels without arousing suspicion.

d) **Data Compression:** Cyber spies use data compression techniques to reduce the size of stolen data before exfiltration, making it easier to transfer large volumes of data over limited bandwidth or network connections. Data compression helps cyber spies minimize the risk of detection and maximize the efficiency of data exfiltration operations.

4. Open-Source Intelligence (OSINT) Gathering:

Open-source intelligence (OSINT) gathering involves collecting information from publicly available sources, such as news articles, social media posts, online forums, and public databases, to gather intelligence about a target's activities, interests, and vulnerabilities. Cyber spies use OSINT gathering techniques, including:

a) **Web Scraping:** Web scraping involves automatically extracting data from websites, social media platforms, or online forums using specialized tools or scripts. Web scraping allows cyber spies to collect large volumes of data quickly and efficiently from publicly accessible sources without manual intervention.

b) **Social Media Monitoring:** Cyber spies monitor social media platforms, such as Facebook, Twitter, and LinkedIn, to gather information about a target's activities, interests, connections, and relationships. Social media monitoring provides valuable insights into the target's personal and professional life, enabling cyber spies to tailor their attacks and social engineering tactics accordingly.

c) **Public Records Searches:** Cyber spies conduct searches of public records, such as property records, court documents, and corporate filings, to gather information about a target's legal history, financial status, or business affiliations. Public records searches provide cyber spies with valuable intelligence for conducting reconnaissance and targeting individuals or organizations.

d) **Dark Web Monitoring:** Cyber spies monitor the dark web, a hidden part of the internet used for illicit activities, to gather intelligence about underground markets, cybercriminal forums, and hacker communities. Dark web monitoring helps cyber spies identify emerging threats, vulnerabilities, and tactics used by malicious actors to target individuals or organizations.

Data collection methods are fundamental to cyber espionage operations, enabling cyber spies to gather valuable intelligence, steal sensitive information, and achieve their objectives. Reconnaissance, social engineering, data exfiltration, and open-source intelligence (OSINT) gathering are among the diverse range of methods used by cyber spies to collect data from their targets. By understanding how cyber spies gather information, individuals, organizations, and governments can better prepare themselves to defend against cyber espionage threats and protect sensitive data and assets from unauthorized access or exploitation. Vigilance, awareness, and cybersecurity measures are essential for mitigating the risks posed by cyber espionage and safeguarding against privacy violations, data breaches, and cyber attacks in the digital age.

Cyber Surveillance

Cyber surveillance is the systematic monitoring, interception, and analysis of digital communications, activities, and behaviors conducted across the internet and other digital networks. It involves the use of various technologies, tools, and techniques to gather intelligence, track online behavior, and collect data for a variety of purposes, including national security, law enforcement, corporate management, marketing, and espionage. Cyber surveillance has become increasingly prevalent in the digital age, driven by advances in technology, the proliferation of digital devices, and the growing volume of data generated and exchanged online. In this section, we'll delve into the different aspects of cyber surveillance, its methods, implications, and controversies.

1. Purpose and Scope of Cyber Surveillance:

Cyber surveillance serves multiple purposes, ranging from monitoring for criminal activities and protecting national security to commercial interests such as targeted advertising and market research. The scope of cyber surveillance extends across various domains, including:

- a) **National Security:** Government agencies and intelligence services conduct cyber surveillance to monitor potential threats to national security, including terrorism, espionage, and cyber attacks. Surveillance programs aim to detect and prevent threats before they materialize, gathering intelligence from digital communications, social media, and online activities.

- b) **Law Enforcement:** Law enforcement agencies use cyber surveillance to investigate criminal activities, gather evidence, and track suspects involved in cybercrimes, such as fraud, identity theft, and online harassment. Surveillance techniques include monitoring communications, tracking online behavior, and intercepting digital data.

- c) **Corporate Management:** Employers and organizations employ cyber surveillance to monitor employees' computer usage, internet activities, and communications for productivity management, security compliance, and regulatory purposes. Surveillance tools may track employee performance, detect insider threats, and enforce acceptable use policies in the workplace.

d) **Marketing and Advertising:** Companies and advertisers use cyber surveillance to collect data on consumer behavior, preferences, and interests for targeted advertising, personalized marketing campaigns, and customer relationship management. Surveillance techniques include tracking online interactions, analyzing browsing habits, and profiling user demographics.

2. Methods of Cyber Surveillance:

Cyber surveillance employs various methods and techniques to monitor, intercept, and collect digital data. These methods include:

a) **Data Interception:** Cyber surveillance involves intercepting digital communications, such as emails, instant messages, and VoIP calls, to monitor content, identify key individuals, and gather intelligence. Surveillance tools may intercept data packets traversing networks, decrypt encrypted communications, or exploit vulnerabilities in communication protocols.

b) **Traffic Analysis:** Surveillance programs analyze network traffic patterns, metadata, and communication protocols to identify trends, behaviors, and relationships between users and devices. Traffic analysis can reveal insights into communication networks, social connections, and organizational structures, aiding in intelligence gathering and threat detection.

c) **Data Collection:** Cyber surveillance collects data from various sources, including websites, social media platforms, mobile apps, and IoT devices. Data collection techniques may involve web scraping, data mining, and API access to extract information from online platforms, databases, and digital repositories.

d) **Social Engineering:** Cyber surveillance uses social engineering tactics, such as phishing, pretexting, and impersonation, to manipulate individuals into revealing sensitive information or granting unauthorized access to systems. Social engineering exploits human psychology, trust, and naivety to deceive targets and gather intelligence.

e) **Technical Exploits:** Cyber surveillance exploits vulnerabilities in software, hardware, and communication protocols to gain unauthorized access to systems, devices, and networks. Exploits may target unpatched software vulnerabilities, weak authentication mechanisms, or misconfigured network settings to infiltrate target environments.

3. **Implications of Cyber Surveillance:**

Cyber surveillance has far-reaching implications for individuals, organizations, and societies, including:

a) **Privacy Concerns:** Cyber surveillance raises significant privacy concerns, as it involves the monitoring, tracking, and analysis of individuals' online activities, communications, and personal information without their consent. Surveillance programs may infringe on privacy rights, undermine civil liberties, and erode trust in digital technologies.

b) **Data Security Risks:** Cyber surveillance introduces data security risks, as intercepted communications, collected data, and surveillance tools may be vulnerable to unauthorized access, interception, or exploitation by malicious actors. Data breaches, leaks, and unauthorized disclosures pose threats to sensitive information and personal privacy.

c) **Civil Liberties:** Cyber surveillance raises questions about civil liberties, free speech, and freedom of expression, as mass surveillance programs may chill public discourse, stifle dissent, and suppress political activism. Surveillance practices may infringe on individual rights to privacy, due process, and protection from unwarranted government intrusion.

d) **Ethical Considerations:** Cyber surveillance raises ethical considerations about the use of surveillance technologies, data collection practices, and the balance between security and individual freedoms. Ethical dilemmas may arise regarding the necessity, proportionality, and legitimacy of surveillance activities in democratic societies.

e) **Legal and Regulatory Frameworks:** Cyber surveillance operates within legal and regulatory frameworks that govern the use of surveillance technologies, data collection practices, and privacy rights. Surveillance laws may vary by jurisdiction, requiring compliance with privacy regulations, transparency requirements, and oversight mechanisms.

4. Controversies and Debates:

Cyber surveillance is a subject of ongoing controversies and debates, including:

a) **Mass Surveillance:** Mass surveillance programs conducted by government agencies have sparked debates about the scope, legality, and proportionality of surveillance practices. Concerns about dragnet surveillance, bulk data collection, and warrantless wiretapping have raised questions about the effectiveness and legitimacy of surveillance programs.

b) **Government Transparency:** Government transparency and accountability are critical issues in the debate over cyber surveillance, as surveillance programs often operate in secrecy, without public oversight or judicial review. Calls for greater transparency, disclosure, and oversight of surveillance activities aim to ensure accountability and safeguard civil liberties.

c) **Surveillance Capitalism:** Surveillance capitalism refers to the commodification of personal data and the monetization of surveillance practices by technology companies and advertisers. Critics argue that surveillance capitalism exploits user privacy, manipulates consumer behavior, and prioritizes profit over individual rights, leading to concerns about data exploitation and algorithmic discrimination.

d) **Digital Rights and Freedoms:** Digital rights and freedoms are at the forefront of debates over cyber surveillance, as individuals demand greater protection of privacy, free speech, and online autonomy in the face of surveillance threats. Advocates for digital rights advocate for stronger privacy laws, encryption protections, and user empowerment tools to safeguard individual freedoms in cyberspace.

Cyber surveillance is a complex and multifaceted phenomenon that encompasses the monitoring, interception, and analysis of digital communications and activities for various purposes. While cyber surveillance plays a crucial role in national security, law enforcement, and corporate management, it also raises significant concerns about privacy, data security, civil liberties, and ethical considerations. Balancing the need for surveillance with respect for individual rights, transparency, and accountability requires careful consideration of legal, ethical, and societal implications in the evolving landscape of digital surveillance.

Exploiting Vulnerabilities

Exploiting vulnerabilities is a fundamental tactic in the realm of cybersecurity, utilized by both defensive and offensive actors. In this section, we'll explore the concept of exploiting vulnerabilities in detail, covering its definition, types of vulnerabilities, methods of exploitation, implications, and strategies for mitigation.

1. Understanding Vulnerabilities:

Vulnerabilities refer to weaknesses or flaws in software, hardware, networks, or systems that can be exploited by attackers to compromise security, gain unauthorized access, or disrupt operations. Vulnerabilities can arise from various sources, including programming errors, design flaws, misconfigurations, or inadequate security controls. Common types of vulnerabilities include:

a) **Software Vulnerabilities:** Software vulnerabilities are flaws or bugs in software applications, operating systems, or firmware that can be exploited to execute arbitrary code, escalate privileges, or compromise system integrity. Examples include buffer overflows, SQL injection, cross-site scripting (XSS), and remote code execution (RCE) vulnerabilities.

b) **Hardware Vulnerabilities:** Hardware vulnerabilities are weaknesses in computer hardware components, such as processors, memory modules, or peripherals, that can be exploited to bypass security controls, extract sensitive information, or tamper with system operations. Examples include speculative execution vulnerabilities, hardware backdoors, and firmware exploits.

c) **Network Vulnerabilities:** Network vulnerabilities are weaknesses in network infrastructure, protocols, or configurations that can be exploited to intercept traffic, conduct man-in-the-middle attacks, or compromise network devices. Examples include weak encryption, insecure protocols, misconfigured firewalls, and unpatched routers.

d) **Human Vulnerabilities:** Human vulnerabilities are weaknesses in human behavior, knowledge, or awareness that can be exploited through social engineering tactics, such as phishing, pretexting, or impersonation, to manipulate individuals into divulging sensitive information or performing unauthorized actions. Examples include password reuse, careless clicking, and trust-based exploitation.

2. Methods of Exploitation:

Exploiting vulnerabilities involves identifying, exploiting, and leveraging weaknesses in target systems or environments to achieve specific objectives. Methods of exploitation vary depending on the type of vulnerability, attacker's capabilities, and target environment, but common techniques include:

a) **Exploit Development:** Exploit development involves creating or adapting software exploits, scripts, or tools to target specific vulnerabilities and gain unauthorized access to systems or networks. Exploits may target known vulnerabilities, zero-day vulnerabilities, or previously undisclosed weaknesses in software or hardware.

b) **Penetration Testing:** Penetration testing, or ethical hacking, involves simulating cyber attacks to identify and exploit vulnerabilities in target systems or networks before malicious actors can exploit them. Penetration testers use a variety of tools and techniques, such as vulnerability scanning, network sniffing, and privilege escalation, to assess security posture and recommend remediation measures.

c) **Social Engineering:** Social engineering tactics involve manipulating human psychology, trust, and behavior to deceive individuals into revealing sensitive information or performing unauthorized actions. Social engineers exploit human vulnerabilities, such as curiosity, fear, or authority, to trick targets into clicking on malicious links, disclosing passwords, or granting access to restricted areas.

d) **Zero-Day Exploitation:** Zero-day exploitation involves exploiting previously unknown vulnerabilities, known as zero-day vulnerabilities, for which no patch or mitigation measures are available. Zero-day exploits are highly sought after by attackers due to their effectiveness and stealthiness, as they bypass detection and evade traditional security controls.

3. Implications of Exploiting Vulnerabilities:

Exploiting vulnerabilities has significant implications for individuals, organizations, and societies, including:

a) **Data Breaches:** Exploiting vulnerabilities can lead to data breaches, where attackers gain unauthorized access to sensitive information, such as personal data, financial records, or intellectual property. Data breaches can result in financial losses, reputational damage, and legal liabilities for affected parties.

b) **Cyber Attacks:** Exploiting vulnerabilities can facilitate cyber attacks, such as malware infections, ransomware attacks, or distributed denial-of-service (DDoS) attacks, which disrupt operations, cause downtime, and compromise system integrity. Cyber attacks can disrupt critical infrastructure, disrupt essential services, and pose threats to national security.

c) **Privacy Violations:** Exploiting vulnerabilities can result in privacy violations, as attackers may intercept communications, eavesdrop on conversations, or monitor online activities without consent. Privacy violations can lead to loss of privacy, intrusion into personal space, and exposure of sensitive information to unauthorized parties.

d) **Financial Losses:** Exploiting vulnerabilities can result in financial losses for individuals, organizations, and governments, as attackers may steal money, extort ransom payments, or engage in fraudulent activities using compromised credentials or financial information. Financial losses can impact business operations, disrupt supply chains, and undermine economic stability.

4. **Mitigation Strategies:**

Mitigating vulnerabilities requires a multi-layered approach that encompasses technical, procedural, and organizational measures to identify, assess, and remediate weaknesses in systems, networks, and processes. Effective mitigation strategies include:

a) **Vulnerability Management:** Implementing vulnerability management programs to identify, prioritize, and remediate vulnerabilities in software, hardware, and systems. Vulnerability management involves vulnerability scanning, patch management, and configuration hardening to reduce the attack surface and minimize the risk of exploitation.

b) **Security Awareness Training:** Providing security awareness training to employees, contractors, and stakeholders to raise awareness about common threats, social engineering tactics, and best practices for protecting against cyber attacks. Security awareness training helps mitigate human vulnerabilities and empower individuals to recognize and report suspicious activities.

c) **Defense-in-Depth:** Implementing defense-in-depth strategies to deploy multiple layers of security controls, such as firewalls, intrusion detection systems (IDS), antivirus software, and endpoint protection, to detect, prevent, and mitigate cyber threats at different stages of the attack lifecycle.

d) **Regular Updates and Patching:** Regularly updating software, firmware, and systems to apply security patches, fixes, and updates released by vendors to address known vulnerabilities and mitigate the risk of exploitation. Patch management processes should be automated, prioritized, and tested to ensure timely remediation of critical vulnerabilities.

e) **Threat Intelligence Sharing:** Sharing threat intelligence and information about emerging threats, attack techniques, and vulnerabilities with trusted partners, industry peers, and cybersecurity communities to enhance situational awareness, threat detection, and incident response capabilities.

Exploiting vulnerabilities is a critical tactic in cybersecurity, used by attackers to compromise security, gain unauthorized access, and achieve malicious objectives. Understanding vulnerabilities, methods of exploitation, implications, and mitigation strategies is essential for individuals, organizations, and governments to effectively defend against cyber threats, protect sensitive information, and safeguard digital assets in the evolving threat landscape of cyberspace. By adopting proactive security measures, implementing best practices, and staying vigilant against emerging threats, stakeholders can mitigate the risks posed by vulnerabilities and enhance resilience against cyber attacks.

Chapter 9
Nations Competing in Cyber Spying

In the digital age, cyberspace has become the new battleground for nations seeking to gain strategic advantages, gather intelligence, and assert dominance in the global arena. With the increasing reliance on digital technologies and interconnected networks, the realm of cyber espionage has emerged as a key domain for nations to compete for political, economic, and military supremacy. In this chapter, we delve into the intricate world of nations competing in cyber spying, exploring the tactics, motivations, and implications of state-sponsored cyber espionage activities.

As governments harness the power of technology to advance their interests and safeguard their national security, cyber spying has become a pervasive and persistent threat in the international landscape. Nation-states engage in cyber espionage operations to gather intelligence, steal intellectual property, disrupt adversaries' operations, and influence geopolitical outcomes. From sophisticated cyber attacks targeting critical infrastructure to covert surveillance operations targeting foreign governments and corporations, nations employ a wide array of tactics and techniques to advance their agendas in cyberspace.

This chapter examines the geopolitical dynamics of cyber spying, the role of state-sponsored actors, and the evolving strategies employed by nations to gain a competitive edge in the digital realm. By understanding the complex interplay of interests, rivalries, and vulnerabilities in cyberspace, stakeholders can better navigate the challenges posed by nation-state cyber threats and safeguard their interests in an increasingly interconnected world.

Global Cyber Powers

Global cyber powers represent nations that wield significant influence and capabilities in the domain of cybersecurity and cyber espionage. These countries possess advanced technological infrastructure, formidable cyber capabilities, and strategic interests that enable them to compete, collaborate, and assert dominance in the global cyberspace. In this section, we'll explore the concept of global cyber powers in detail, examining the key players, their capabilities, motivations, and implications for international security.

1. **Key Players in Global Cyber Powers:**

    a) **United States:** The United States is widely recognized as a global leader in cyber capabilities, with extensive investments in cybersecurity research, development, and operations. The U.S. government, military, and intelligence agencies maintain sophisticated cyber capabilities for offensive and defensive purposes, including espionage, sabotage, and deterrence. The National Security Agency (NSA), Cyber Command (CYBERCOM), and other agencies play pivotal roles in conducting cyber operations, defending critical infrastructure, and countering cyber threats.

    b) **China:** China has emerged as a formidable cyber power, with significant investments in cyber warfare capabilities, offensive cyber operations, and cyber espionage activities. The Chinese government, military, and state-sponsored hackers engage in cyber operations to advance national interests, gather intelligence, and exert influence in cyberspace. The People's Liberation Army (PLA) and Ministry of State Security (MSS) are key actors in China's cyber strategy, focusing on economic espionage, intellectual property theft, and geopolitical espionage.

c) **Russia:** Russia is another major player in global cyber powers, known for its sophisticated cyber capabilities, aggressive cyber operations, and strategic use of cyber tools for political purposes. The Russian government, military, and intelligence agencies conduct cyber operations to undermine adversaries, disrupt democratic processes, and assert influence in international affairs. The Federal Security Service (FSB), Main Intelligence Directorate (GRU), and various state-sponsored hacking groups, such as Fancy Bear and Cozy Bear, are instrumental in Russia's cyber activities.

d) **Israel:** Israel is a prominent player in the global cyber landscape, renowned for its advanced cybersecurity industry, innovative technologies, and proactive approach to cyber defense and offense. The Israeli government, military, and intelligence agencies invest heavily in cybersecurity research, development, and operations to counter threats from hostile actors, protect critical infrastructure, and maintain technological superiority. The Israel Defense Forces (IDF), Mossad, and Unit 8200 are key players in Israel's cyber strategy, focusing on intelligence gathering, cyber warfare, and counterterrorism operations.

e) **United Kingdom:** The United Kingdom is a significant player in global cyber powers, with robust capabilities in cybersecurity, intelligence gathering, and offensive cyber operations. The British government, military, and intelligence agencies collaborate closely to defend against cyber threats, conduct cyber espionage, and support national security objectives. The Government Communications Headquarters (GCHQ), Ministry of Defence (MoD), and

National Cyber Security Centre (NCSC) play pivotal roles in the UK's cyber defense and intelligence operations.

2. Capabilities of Global Cyber Powers:

Global cyber powers possess diverse capabilities in cybersecurity, cyber warfare, and cyber espionage, including:

a) **Advanced Cyber Tools:** Global cyber powers develop and deploy advanced cyber tools, malware, and exploits for conducting offensive cyber operations, infiltrating target networks, and collecting intelligence. These tools include sophisticated malware strains, such as Stuxnet, Duqu, and Flame, as well as custom-built exploits targeting specific vulnerabilities in software, hardware, or networks.

b) **Cyber Intelligence Gathering:** Global cyber powers leverage extensive signals intelligence (SIGINT) capabilities, covert surveillance techniques, and cyber espionage operations to gather intelligence from adversaries, allies, and targets of interest. Cyber intelligence encompasses the collection, analysis, and exploitation of digital communications, data, and information to support national security objectives, military operations, and diplomatic initiatives.

c) **Strategic Cyber Operations:** Global cyber powers conduct strategic cyber operations to achieve political, military, and economic objectives in cyberspace. These operations may involve disrupting adversaries' critical infrastructure, sabotaging military systems, or influencing public opinion through cyber propaganda and disinformation campaigns. Strategic cyber operations aim to shape geopolitical dynamics, deter adversaries, and project national power in the digital domain.

d) **Defensive Cyber Capabilities:** Global cyber powers invest in defensive cybersecurity measures, resilience-building efforts, and incident response capabilities to defend against cyber threats, mitigate risks, and protect critical infrastructure from cyber attacks. Defensive measures include network security, endpoint protection, threat detection, and incident response protocols to detect, contain, and neutralize cyber threats in real-time.

3. **Motivations for Global Cyber Powers:**

Global cyber powers are motivated by various factors to develop, enhance, and wield cyber capabilities, including:

   a) **National Security:** Protecting national security interests is a primary motivation for global cyber powers, as cyber capabilities enable governments to defend against external threats, deter adversaries, and maintain strategic superiority in cyberspace.

   b) **Economic Espionage:** Global cyber powers engage in economic espionage activities to steal intellectual property, proprietary information, and trade secrets from foreign competitors to gain economic advantages, enhance competitiveness, and promote national interests.

   c) **Geopolitical Influence:** Cyber capabilities are used by global cyber powers to exert influence, project power, and advance geopolitical agendas in the international arena. Cyber operations enable governments to shape narratives, manipulate public opinion, and influence decision-making processes in target countries.

   d) **Military Superiority:** Achieving military superiority is a key objective for global cyber powers, as cyber capabilities play a critical role in modern warfare, intelligence gathering, and military operations. Cyber operations enable governments to disrupt adversaries' military systems, sabotage critical infrastructure, and gain tactical advantages on the battlefield.

4. **Implications of Global Cyber Powers:**

The presence of global cyber powers has significant implications for international security, diplomatic relations, and the global economy, including:

   a) **Cyber Arms Race:** The proliferation of cyber capabilities among global powers has led to a cyber arms race, where nations compete to develop, acquire, and deploy advanced cyber tools and technologies to gain strategic advantages in cyberspace.

   b) **Cyber Conflict:** The rivalry between global cyber powers has increased the likelihood of cyber conflicts, where nations engage in offensive cyber operations, espionage activities, and sabotage campaigns to achieve political, military, or economic objectives.

   c) **Escalation Risks:** The escalation of cyber conflicts between global powers poses risks of unintended consequences, including retaliation, escalation, and unintended damage to critical infrastructure, civilian populations, and international stability.

   d) **Diplomatic Tensions:** Cyber incidents involving global cyber powers can strain diplomatic relations, trigger international tensions, and undermine trust between nations, leading to diplomatic crises, sanctions, and retaliatory measures.

e) **Economic Impacts:** Cyber espionage activities conducted by global cyber powers can have significant economic impacts, including loss of intellectual property, disruption of supply chains, and damage to businesses and industries targeted by cyber attacks.

Global cyber powers represent nations with significant influence, capabilities, and interests in the domain of cybersecurity and cyber espionage. These countries leverage advanced technologies, strategic partnerships, and covert operations to compete, collaborate, and assert dominance in the global cyberspace. Understanding the motivations, capabilities, and implications of global cyber powers is essential for addressing cyber threats, promoting international cooperation, and safeguarding the security and stability of cyberspace in an increasingly interconnected world.

Cyber Arms Race

The cyber arms race refers to the ongoing competition between nations, organizations, and individuals to develop, acquire, and deploy advanced cyber capabilities for offensive and defensive purposes. In this section, we'll delve into the concept of the cyber arms race, exploring its origins, key players, tactics, implications, and strategies for managing and mitigating the risks associated with cyber warfare and cyber conflict.

1. Origins of the Cyber Arms Race:

The origins of the cyber arms race can be traced back to the early days of the internet and the emergence of cyber warfare as a new domain of conflict. As nations recognized the strategic importance of cyberspace for national security, economic competitiveness, and geopolitical influence, they began investing in cyber capabilities to gain a competitive edge in the digital domain. The proliferation of cyber attacks, espionage activities, and disruptive cyber operations fueled the escalation of the cyber arms race, as governments sought to develop offensive cyber capabilities to counter emerging threats and defend against cyber attacks from adversaries.

2. **Key Players in the Cyber Arms Race:**

    a) **Nation-States:** Nation-states are primary players in the cyber arms race, investing significant resources in cyber warfare capabilities, offensive cyber operations, and cyber espionage activities to advance national security interests, protect critical infrastructure, and project power in cyberspace. Leading cyber powers, such as the United States, China, Russia, Israel, and the United Kingdom, maintain formidable cyber capabilities and conduct sophisticated cyber operations to achieve political, military, and economic objectives.

    b) **State-Sponsored Actors:** State-sponsored actors, including government agencies, intelligence services, and military units, play a central role in the cyber arms race, conducting cyber espionage, sabotage, and disruption campaigns on behalf of their respective governments. These actors leverage advanced cyber tools, techniques, and infrastructure to gather intelligence, infiltrate target networks, and execute covert cyber operations against adversaries.

    c) **Cybercriminal Groups:** Cybercriminal groups also contribute to the cyber arms race by developing and deploying cyber weapons, malware, and exploits for financial gain, political motives, or ideological purposes. These groups engage in cyber attacks, ransomware campaigns, and data breaches to steal sensitive information, extort victims, and disrupt operations for profit or political leverage.

d) **Hacktivist Collectives:** Hacktivist collectives, such as Anonymous and Lizard Squad, participate in the cyber arms race by launching cyber attacks, defacing websites, and disrupting online services to promote social or political causes, raise awareness about issues, or protest against perceived injustices. While hacktivists may lack the resources and sophistication of nation-states, they can still pose significant disruptions and reputational damage to targeted entities.

3. **Tactics and Techniques in the Cyber Arms Race:**

The cyber arms race encompasses a wide range of tactics and techniques employed by adversaries to gain advantage, inflict harm, and achieve strategic objectives in cyberspace, including:

a) **Cyber Espionage:** Cyber espionage involves infiltrating target networks, stealing sensitive information, and conducting covert surveillance operations to gather intelligence, monitor adversaries' activities, and gain strategic insights into their capabilities, intentions, and vulnerabilities. Cyber espionage tactics include phishing, malware implants, data exfiltration, and social engineering to access and exfiltrate valuable data from target systems.

b) **Cyber Attacks:** Cyber attacks encompass a broad spectrum of offensive operations, ranging from disruptive cyber attacks targeting critical infrastructure, such as power grids, transportation networks, and financial systems, to destructive attacks aiming to cause physical damage, disrupt operations, and undermine confidence in the targeted organization or government. Cyber attacks may involve malware infections, ransomware campaigns, distributed denial-of-service (DDoS) attacks, and supply chain compromises to achieve desired effects.

c) **Cyber Warfare:** Cyber warfare involves the use of offensive cyber capabilities by nation-states to conduct military operations, disrupt adversaries' military systems, and achieve strategic objectives in conflict scenarios. Cyber warfare tactics include targeting command and control systems, disrupting communications networks, and sabotaging critical infrastructure to degrade adversaries' capabilities, disrupt operations, and gain tactical advantages on the battlefield.

d) **Information Operations:** Information operations encompass propaganda, disinformation, and psychological warfare tactics aimed at influencing public opinion, shaping narratives, and manipulating perceptions in cyberspace. Information operations may involve spreading fake news, conducting influence campaigns, and manipulating social media platforms to sway public opinion, undermine trust in institutions, and destabilize target societies.

4. **Implications of the Cyber Arms Race:**

The cyber arms race has significant implications for national security, international relations, and global stability, including:

a) **Escalation Risks:** The escalation of the cyber arms race poses risks of unintended consequences, including retaliatory cyber attacks, escalation of hostilities, and unintended damage to critical infrastructure, civilian populations, and international stability. Misattributed cyber attacks, false flag operations, and the proliferation of cyber weapons can exacerbate tensions and increase the likelihood of cyber conflict.

b) **Geopolitical Tensions:** The cyber arms race contributes to geopolitical tensions and rivalries among nations, as governments vie for dominance, influence, and control in the digital domain. Competing interests, strategic imperatives, and divergent cyber capabilities can fuel mistrust, suspicion, and rivalry between global powers, leading to diplomatic standoffs, economic sanctions, and cyber-related incidents.

c) **Economic Impacts:** The cyber arms race has economic impacts on governments, industries, and societies, including the costs of cyber defense, incident response, and recovery from cyber attacks. Economic espionage, intellectual property theft, and disruption of critical infrastructure can result in financial losses, market instability, and erosion of confidence in the digital economy.

d) **Cyber Arms Proliferation:** The proliferation of cyber weapons, exploits, and malware in the cyber arms race raises concerns about their misuse, proliferation, and unintended consequences. Cyber weapons developed by nation-states can be stolen, leaked, or sold to non-state actors, terrorist organizations, or rogue states, increasing the risk of cyber attacks, sabotage, and destabilization in cyberspace.

5. **Strategies for Managing the Cyber Arms Race:**

Managing the cyber arms race requires a multi-dimensional approach that encompasses diplomatic, legal, technological, and strategic measures to reduce tensions, promote cooperation, and mitigate risks in cyberspace, including:

a) **International Cooperation:** Strengthening international cooperation and collaboration among governments, industry stakeholders, and cybersecurity experts to develop norms, standards, and protocols for responsible behavior in cyberspace, enhance information sharing, and build trust between nations.

b) **Cyber Deterrence:** Establishing credible deterrence strategies, including declaratory policies, attribution capabilities, and proportional responses to cyber attacks, to deter adversaries from engaging in malicious cyber activities and to impose costs for violations of international norms and laws.

c) **Cyber Resilience:** Enhancing cyber resilience through investments in cybersecurity infrastructure, workforce training, incident response capabilities, and resilience-building measures to mitigate the impact of cyber attacks, minimize disruptions, and recover rapidly from cyber incidents.

d) **Norms and Rules of Engagement:** Developing and promoting norms, rules of engagement, and international agreements to govern state behavior in cyberspace, clarify acceptable conduct, and establish red lines for cyber operations to prevent misunderstandings, miscalculations, and escalations in the cyber domain.

e) **Capacity Building:** Building cybersecurity capacity and capabilities in developing countries, emerging economies, and regions with limited resources to improve cyber defenses, enhance cyber hygiene practices, and strengthen resilience against cyber threats, contributing to global stability and security.

The cyber arms race represents a complex and dynamic competition between nations, organizations, and individuals to develop, acquire, and deploy advanced cyber capabilities for offensive and defensive purposes. Understanding the origins, key players, tactics, implications, and strategies for managing the cyber arms race is essential for addressing the challenges posed by cyber warfare, promoting international cooperation, and safeguarding the security and stability of cyberspace in an increasingly interconnected world. By adopting proactive measures, enhancing cyber resilience, and promoting responsible behavior in cyberspace, stakeholders can mitigate the risks associated with the cyber arms race and foster a safer, more secure digital environment for all.

The Impact on International Relations

The impact of the cyber arms race on international relations is profound and multifaceted, influencing diplomatic dynamics, strategic calculations, and global stability in the digital age. As nations compete for dominance, influence, and control in cyberspace, the evolving landscape of cyber warfare, espionage, and conflict reshapes traditional notions of security, sovereignty, and cooperation among states. In this section, we'll explore the impact of the cyber arms race on international relations in detail, examining its implications for state behavior, diplomatic interactions, and the rules-based order in cyberspace.

1. Shifting Power Dynamics:

The cyber arms race has altered the traditional power dynamics among nations, as cyber capabilities become increasingly vital for national security, economic competitiveness, and geopolitical influence. States with advanced cyber capabilities, such as the United States, China, Russia, and Israel, wield significant influence in shaping the global agenda, projecting power in cyberspace, and shaping the norms and rules governing state behavior in the digital domain. Emerging cyber powers, such as India, Brazil, and South Korea, are also vying for prominence in the cyber arms race, leveraging their technological prowess and strategic partnerships to enhance their cyber capabilities and assert their interests on the international stage.

2. Erosion of Trust and Cooperation:

The cyber arms race has eroded trust and cooperation among nations, as suspicions of cyber espionage, sabotage, and subversion undermine diplomatic relations, bilateral agreements, and multilateral efforts to address common challenges in cyberspace. Incidents of state-sponsored cyber attacks, data breaches, and disinformation campaigns have heightened tensions between rival powers, fueling a climate of mistrust, suspicion, and recrimination in diplomatic interactions. Efforts to promote international cooperation, information sharing, and confidence-building measures in cyberspace are often stymied by divergent interests, conflicting priorities, and concerns about sovereignty, privacy, and national security.

3. Cyber Diplomacy and Norm Development:

The cyber arms race has spurred efforts to develop norms, rules of engagement, and diplomatic mechanisms to manage cyber conflicts, reduce the risks of escalation, and promote responsible behavior among states in cyberspace. Diplomatic initiatives, such as the United Nations Group of Governmental Experts (UN GGE) on Developments in the Field of Information and Telecommunications in the Context of International Security and the Budapest Convention on Cybercrime, seek to establish common principles, norms, and standards for state behavior in cyberspace, including the prohibition of cyber attacks against critical infrastructure, respect for sovereignty and human rights, and cooperation on cybersecurity capacity building and incident response.

4. Deterrence and Strategic Stability:

The cyber arms race has raised questions about deterrence and strategic stability in the digital age, as nations grapple with the challenges of deterring cyber attacks, attributing responsibility for cyber incidents, and imposing costs for violations of international norms and laws in cyberspace. Traditional concepts of deterrence, such as mutually assured destruction (MAD), are ill-suited to the cyber domain, where attribution is difficult, offensive cyber capabilities are proliferating, and the threshold for escalation is ambiguous. States are exploring new approaches to cyber deterrence, including declaratory policies, cyber doctrines, and retaliatory measures, to signal resolve, impose consequences, and shape adversaries' calculus in cyberspace.

5. Geopolitical Competition and Influence Operations:

The cyber arms race has intensified geopolitical competition and influence operations in cyberspace, as nations vie for strategic advantages, undermine rivals' interests, and shape narratives to advance their geopolitical agendas. State-sponsored actors engage in cyber espionage, disinformation campaigns, and psychological warfare tactics to influence public opinion, manipulate perceptions, and undermine trust in democratic institutions, electoral processes, and international organizations. The weaponization of information and the spread of fake news in cyberspace have heightened concerns about the erosion of democratic norms, the rise of authoritarian regimes, and the destabilization of global governance structures.

6. Cyber Conflict and Escalation Risks:

The cyber arms race has increased the risks of cyber conflict and escalation among nations, as offensive cyber capabilities proliferate, cyber operations become more sophisticated, and adversaries exploit vulnerabilities in cyberspace to achieve strategic objectives. Escalation dynamics in cyberspace are complex and unpredictable, with cyber attacks having the potential to trigger retaliatory measures, military responses, and cascading effects that escalate tensions and undermine stability in the international system. Misattributed cyber attacks, false flag operations, and the proliferation of cyber weapons raise concerns about the risks of inadvertent escalation and unintended consequences in the cyber domain.

7. Global Governance Challenges:

The cyber arms race poses significant challenges for global governance, as existing frameworks, institutions, and norms struggle to keep pace with the rapid evolution of cyberspace and the proliferation of cyber threats. Efforts to develop international norms, rules of engagement, and mechanisms for cyber cooperation face obstacles, including divergent interests, competing priorities, and the lack of consensus among states on key issues such as attribution, sovereignty, and the applicability of international law in cyberspace. Bridging the gap between state interests, industry perspectives, and civil society concerns remains a formidable challenge for policymakers, diplomats, and cybersecurity experts seeking to promote a rules-based order in cyberspace.

The cyber arms race has far-reaching implications for international relations, shaping the behavior of states, influencing diplomatic interactions, and reshaping the global order in the digital age. Addressing the challenges posed by the cyber arms race requires concerted efforts to promote trust, cooperation, and responsible behavior among nations, strengthen diplomatic mechanisms, and develop norms, rules, and institutions for managing cyber conflicts and promoting stability in cyberspace. By fostering dialogue, building consensus, and enhancing resilience against cyber threats, stakeholders can mitigate the risks associated with the cyber arms race and promote a safer, more secure digital environment for all.

Chapter 10
Exploring the Dark Web

The dark web is a mysterious and enigmatic realm of the internet, shrouded in secrecy and intrigue. Unlike the surface web, which comprises websites accessible through traditional search engines, the dark web exists on encrypted networks that require special software, configurations, or permissions to access. In this chapter, we embark on a journey to explore the dark web, delving into its origins, structure, activities, and implications for cybersecurity and society.

The dark web has gained notoriety as a haven for illicit activities, including the sale of drugs, weapons, stolen data, and other contraband, facilitated by anonymous cryptocurrencies and encrypted communication tools. However, beyond its criminal underbelly, the dark web also serves as a refuge for whistleblowers, dissidents, and individuals seeking privacy and anonymity in an era of pervasive surveillance and digital tracking.

Through our exploration of the dark web, we aim to demystify its complexities, shed light on its dual nature as both a hub of criminality and a bastion of privacy, and examine the challenges and opportunities it presents for law enforcement, policymakers, and cybersecurity professionals. By understanding the dark web's inner workings, participants, and implications, we can better navigate its risks, harness its potential, and safeguard the integrity and security of the internet for all users.

What is the Dark Web?

The dark web is a hidden and encrypted part of the internet that is not indexed by traditional search engines and is only accessible through specific software, configurations, or permissions. Unlike the surface web, which comprises websites and content that are readily accessible to the general public, the dark web exists on overlay networks that require specialized tools, such as the Tor browser, I2P, or Freenet, to access. In this section, we'll delve into the intricacies of the dark web, exploring its structure, characteristics, activities, and implications for cybersecurity and society.

1. Origins and Structure:

The origins of the dark web can be traced back to the development of anonymizing technologies, such as Tor (The Onion Router), which was originally created by the U.S. Navy for secure communication and anonymity online. Tor works by encrypting and routing internet traffic through a series of relays, or nodes, to conceal users' IP addresses and locations, making it difficult for third parties to track their online activities. Other anonymizing networks, such as I2P (Invisible Internet Project) and Freenet, offer similar capabilities for anonymity and censorship resistance.

The dark web comprises websites, forums, marketplaces, and communication channels that operate on these anonymizing networks, allowing users to browse, publish, and communicate anonymously. These websites often have ".onion" domains and are accessible only through Tor or other dark web access tools. The decentralized and distributed nature of the dark web makes it resistant to censorship and surveillance, enabling users to bypass internet restrictions, evade government surveillance, and access content that may be illegal or prohibited in their countries.

2. Activities and Content:

The dark web hosts a wide range of activities and content, spanning legal, illicit, and controversial domains. While not all activity on the dark web is illegal or harmful, it has gained notoriety as a hub for illicit activities due to its anonymity features and lack of oversight. Some common activities and content found on the dark web include:

a) **Marketplaces:** The dark web hosts numerous online marketplaces where users can buy and sell a variety of goods and services anonymously, including drugs, weapons, counterfeit currency, stolen data, hacking tools, and forged documents. These marketplaces often use cryptocurrencies, such as Bitcoin and Monero, for transactions to preserve anonymity and evade law enforcement.

b) **Forums and Communities:** There are forums and communities on the dark web dedicated to a wide range of topics, including cybersecurity, privacy, politics, activism, and whistleblowing. These forums provide a platform for users to discuss sensitive or controversial issues, share information, and organize activities without fear of censorship or surveillance.

c) **Whistleblower Platforms:** The dark web hosts whistleblower platforms, such as Secure Drop and Global Leaks, where individuals can anonymously submit sensitive information, documents, or tips to journalists, activists, or organizations without revealing their identities. These platforms play a crucial role in exposing corruption, abuse of power, and wrongdoing while protecting whistleblowers from retaliation.

d) **Criminal Services:** Some websites on the dark web offer criminal services, such as hacking services, DDoS (Distributed Denial of Service) attacks, ransomware-as-a-service, and money laundering services, for a fee. These services enable cybercriminals to carry out malicious activities, exploit vulnerabilities, and profit from illicit activities with relative impunity.

e) **Controversial Content:** The dark web also hosts controversial and illegal content, including child exploitation material, extremist propaganda, illegal pornography, and graphic violence. While the dark web provides anonymity and privacy for users, it also serves as a platform for individuals and groups to engage in harmful or illegal activities away from the scrutiny of law enforcement and authorities.

3. **Implications for Cybersecurity and Society:**

The proliferation of illicit activities and malicious actors on the dark web poses significant challenges for cybersecurity, law enforcement, and society at large. Some key implications include:

a) **Cybercrime:** The dark web facilitates cybercrime by providing a platform for cybercriminals to buy, sell, and exchange goods and services anonymously. Cybercriminals use the dark web to trade stolen data, distribute malware, and orchestrate cyber attacks, making it difficult for law enforcement to identify and apprehend perpetrators.

b) **Privacy and Anonymity:** While the dark web offers privacy and anonymity for users, it also attracts individuals seeking to engage in illicit or harmful activities without accountability. The anonymity provided by the dark web can be exploited by criminals, terrorists, and malicious actors to evade detection, conceal their identities, and carry out nefarious activities with impunity.

c) **Challenges for Law Enforcement:** Law enforcement agencies face significant challenges in monitoring, investigating, and combating criminal activities on the dark web. The decentralized and encrypted nature of the dark web makes it difficult to trace users, identify perpetrators, and gather evidence for prosecution. Traditional law enforcement methods may be ineffective against cybercriminals operating on the dark web, requiring innovative approaches and international cooperation to address emerging threats.

d) **Censorship Resistance:** The dark web provides a platform for individuals living in repressive regimes or facing internet censorship to access information, communicate freely, and exercise their rights to privacy and freedom of expression. However, the anonymity of the dark web also enables malicious actors to disseminate propaganda, extremist ideologies, and illegal content without accountability, posing challenges for content moderation and combating online radicalization.

e) **Ethical Considerations:** The dark web raises ethical considerations regarding the balance between privacy, freedom of expression, and law enforcement interests. While anonymity can protect whistleblowers, activists, and dissidents from persecution and reprisals, it can also enable criminal activities, exploitation, and abuse. Finding the right balance between privacy rights and law enforcement needs is essential for safeguarding civil liberties while combating illicit activities on the dark web.

4. Mitigating Risks and Enhancing Security:

Mitigating the risks associated with the dark web requires a multi-faceted approach that involves collaboration between governments, law enforcement agencies, technology companies, and civil society organizations. Some strategies for enhancing security and mitigating risks on the dark web include:

a) **Law Enforcement Cooperation:** Enhancing international cooperation and information sharing among law enforcement agencies to investigate cybercrime, disrupt criminal networks, and prosecute perpetrators operating on the dark web.

b) **Technological Solutions:** Developing and deploying advanced technologies, such as machine learning, blockchain analysis, and encryption algorithms, to identify and track illicit activities, monitor dark web marketplaces, and enhance cybersecurity defenses against emerging threats.

c) **Education and Awareness:** Raising public awareness about the risks and dangers of the dark web, educating users about cybersecurity best practices, and promoting digital literacy to empower individuals to navigate the online world safely and responsibly.

d) **Regulatory Measures:** Implementing regulatory measures and policies to combat cybercrime, protect consumers, and hold dark web operators accountable for facilitating illegal activities, such as drug trafficking, human trafficking, and child exploitation.

e) **Ethical Considerations:** Promoting ethical behavior and responsible use of anonymizing technologies, such as Tor and cryptocurrencies, to uphold privacy rights, freedom of expression, and democratic values while preventing abuse and exploitation by malicious actors.

The dark web is a complex and multifaceted phenomenon that presents both opportunities and challenges for cybersecurity, law enforcement, and society. While it offers privacy, anonymity, and censorship resistance for individuals seeking to exercise their rights online, it also harbors criminal activities, illicit markets, and harmful content that pose risks to individuals and communities. By understanding the structure, activities, and implications of the dark web, stakeholders can develop strategies and measures to mitigate risks, enhance security, and promote a safer, more secure online environment for all users.

Cyber Spying on the Dark Web

Cyber spying on the dark web represents a significant and evolving threat to individuals, organizations, and governments worldwide. As a clandestine and covert activity conducted in the shadows of the internet, cyber spying encompasses a range of tactics, techniques, and operations aimed at infiltrating, monitoring, and extracting sensitive information from target networks, systems, and individuals. In this section, we'll explore the landscape of cyber spying on the dark web, including its methods, motivations, actors, and implications for cybersecurity and national security.

1. **Methods of Cyber Spying:**

Cyber spying on the dark web employs a variety of methods and techniques to gather intelligence, surveil targets, and exfiltrate sensitive information. Some common methods include:

a) **Malware and Exploits:** Cyber spies deploy malware, such as remote access Trojans (RATs), key loggers, and spyware, to infiltrate target systems, compromise devices, and steal data covertly. These malware payloads are often delivered through phishing emails, malicious attachments, or compromised websites, allowing attackers to maintain persistence and conduct surveillance undetected.

b) **Social Engineering:** Cyber spies use social engineering tactics, such as phishing, pretexting, and baiting, to manipulate individuals into divulging sensitive information or granting unauthorized access to their accounts or systems. By impersonating trusted entities or exploiting psychological vulnerabilities, attackers can deceive victims and gain access to valuable intelligence.

c) **Hacking and Intrusions:** Cyber spies leverage hacking techniques, such as network scanning, password cracking, and SQL injection, to breach target networks, servers, and databases. Once inside a target environment, attackers can move laterally, escalate privileges, and exfiltrate sensitive data without detection, exploiting vulnerabilities and misconfigurations to evade detection.

d) **Zero-Day Exploits:** Cyber spies exploit zero-day vulnerabilities, software flaws, and undisclosed weaknesses in operating systems, applications, and hardware to conduct targeted attacks and gain unauthorized access to systems. Zero-day exploits are highly prized by cyber espionage groups and state-sponsored actors due to their effectiveness and stealthy nature.

e) **Cryptography and Encryption:** Cyber spies use cryptography and encryption techniques to secure their communications, hide their activities, and protect sensitive information from interception or surveillance. Encrypted messaging apps, anonymous email services, and secure communication protocols enable attackers to communicate covertly and evade detection by law enforcement and intelligence agencies.

2. **Motivations for Cyber Spying:**

Cyber spying on the dark web is driven by a range of motivations, including espionage, intelligence gathering, competitive advantage, and ideological or political objectives. Some common motivations include:

a) **State-Sponsored Espionage:** Nation-states engage in cyber spying to gather intelligence, monitor adversaries, and advance their strategic interests in cyberspace. State-sponsored cyber espionage operations target government agencies, military institutions, defense contractors, and critical infrastructure sectors to steal classified information, intellectual property, and military secrets.

b) **Corporate Espionage:** Competing businesses and industry rivals engage in cyber spying to gain competitive advantage, steal trade secrets, and sabotage their competitors. Corporate espionage operations target companies, research institutions, and technology firms to obtain proprietary information, customer data, and research and development plans.

c) **Political Intelligence:** Political actors and nation-states conduct cyber spying to monitor political opponents, dissidents, and activists, gather compromising information, and influence election outcomes. Political intelligence operations target political parties, government officials, journalists, and civil society organizations to manipulate public opinion and undermine democratic processes.

d) **Cyber Warfare:** Cyber spies may engage in cyber warfare activities, such as sabotage, disruption, and propaganda, to undermine the security and stability of rival nations, sow discord, and achieve geopolitical objectives. Cyber warfare operations target critical infrastructure, financial systems, and government networks to cause disruption, economic damage, and political instability.

e) **Ideological Motivations:** Cyber spies with ideological or extremist agendas may conduct cyber espionage operations to promote their beliefs, spread propaganda, and recruit followers. Ideologically motivated cyber spies target government institutions, religious organizations, and cultural institutions to advance their agendas and undermine perceived enemies.

3. **Actors and Organizations:**

Cyber spying on the dark web is perpetrated by a diverse range of actors, including nation-states, intelligence agencies, criminal organizations, hacktivist groups, and cyber mercenaries. Some notable actors and organizations involved in cyber spying include:

a) **Nation-State Actors:** Nation-states engage in cyber espionage to gather intelligence, monitor adversaries, and advance their strategic interests. Countries such as Russia, China, Iran, North Korea, and the United States have sophisticated cyber capabilities and conduct cyber spying operations to maintain their geopolitical dominance and influence.

b) **Intelligence Agencies:** Government intelligence agencies, such as the NSA (National Security Agency), CIA (Central Intelligence Agency), GCHQ (Government Communications Headquarters), and Mossad, conduct cyber spying operations to collect signals intelligence, monitor communications, and gather information on foreign adversaries.

c) **Cybercriminal Organizations:** Cybercriminal groups, including advanced persistent threats (APTs), cybercrime syndicates, and organized crime rings, engage in cyber spying for financial gain, theft of intellectual property, and extortion. These groups may sell stolen data on the dark web, engage in corporate espionage, or conduct ransomware attacks to monetize their activities.

d) **Hacktivist Groups:** Hacktivist collectives, such as Anonymous, LulzSec, and APT28 (Fancy Bear), conduct cyber spying operations to promote political or social causes, expose corruption, and challenge authority. Hacktivists may target government agencies, corporations, and institutions they perceive as oppressive or unjust, using hacking techniques to disrupt operations and expose sensitive information.

e) **Private Contractors:** Private cybersecurity firms and contractors may provide cyber espionage services to government clients, intelligence agencies, or corporate clients seeking to gather intelligence, conduct surveillance, or monitor competitors. These contractors may possess specialized expertise, tools, and capabilities for conducting cyber spying operations discreetly and effectively.

4. **Implications for Cybersecurity and National Security:**

Cyber spying on the dark web poses significant implications for cybersecurity, national security, and global stability, including:

a) **Data Breaches and Loss of Intellectual Property:** Cyber spying operations result in data breaches, theft of intellectual property, and compromise of sensitive information, leading to financial losses, reputational damage, and loss of competitive advantage for targeted organizations.

b) **Erosion of Trust and Diplomatic Relations:** Cyber spying erodes trust between nations, undermines diplomatic relations, and escalates tensions in the international community. Revelations of state-sponsored cyber espionage activities can strain diplomatic ties, trigger sanctions, and provoke retaliatory measures, destabilizing global security and stability.

c) **Threats to Critical Infrastructure:** Cyber spying poses threats to critical infrastructure sectors, such as energy, transportation, and healthcare, by targeting industrial control systems, operational technology, and internet-connected devices. Cyber spies may exploit vulnerabilities in critical infrastructure to disrupt operations, cause physical damage, or steal sensitive data, posing risks to public safety and national security.

d) **Cyber Arms Race and Escalation Risks:** Cyber spying fuels a global cyber arms race, as nations invest in cyber capabilities, develop offensive cyber weapons, and engage in offensive operations to gain strategic advantage in cyberspace. The proliferation of cyber weapons and escalation risks increase the likelihood of cyber conflicts, retaliation, and unintended consequences, raising concerns about international security and stability.

e) **Challenges for Law Enforcement and Intelligence Agencies:** Cyber spying presents challenges for law enforcement and intelligence agencies tasked with monitoring, investigating, and countering cyber threats. The anonymous and decentralized nature of the dark web complicates attribution, evidence collection, and prosecution of cyber spies, requiring enhanced cooperation, resources, and expertise to address emerging threats effectively.

5. Mitigating Cyber Spying Risks:

Addressing the risks associated with cyber spying on the dark web requires a multi-faceted approach that involves collaboration between governments, private sector entities, cybersecurity experts, and international organizations. Some strategies for mitigating cyber spying risks include:

a) **Enhanced Cybersecurity Measures:** Implementing robust cybersecurity measures, such as network segmentation, encryption, and multi-factor authentication, to protect against intrusions, data breaches, and unauthorized access by cyber spies.

b) **Threat Intelligence Sharing:** Sharing threat intelligence and cyber threat indicators among government agencies, private sector organizations, and international partners to identify and counter cyber espionage activities effectively.

c) **Diplomatic Engagement and Norms:** Engaging in diplomatic dialogue and cooperation to establish international norms, rules, and agreements governing state behavior in cyberspace and promoting responsible conduct to reduce the risk of cyber conflicts and escalation.

d) **Regulatory Frameworks and Accountability:** Developing and enforcing regulatory frameworks, laws, and international treaties to hold cyber spies accountable for their actions, deter malicious behavior, and promote responsible behavior in cyberspace.

e) **Investment in Cyber Resilience:** Investing in cyber resilience, incident response capabilities, and cyber insurance to mitigate the impact of cyber espionage attacks, recover from breaches, and protect critical assets and infrastructure from persistent threats.

Cyber spying on the dark web represents a complex and evolving challenge for cybersecurity, national security, and global stability. By understanding the methods, motivations, actors, and implications of cyber espionage activities, stakeholders can develop strategies and measures to mitigate risks, enhance security, and safeguard the integrity and stability of cyberspace for all users.